CONTENTS

PREFACE

Sri Gurubhyo Namaha

My sincere pranams and salutations to all my bosses who gave me insight into the Dos and Don'ts of management during my interesting and exciting career. I also wish to express my gratitude to those leaders for giving me an opportunity to work in their respective organizations.

There are different approaches to learning, a) Reading books, b) Personal experience in various situations and c) Others' experiences. Through this book, I would like to use the last approach and share learnings from my own experience gathered in an exciting career of 35 years.

It had always been my son and daughter who were pushing me to write a book on my diversified experience in manufacturing. They wanted me to share my knowledge broadly and professionally since I used to share with them many such experiences, and they would find it highly inspiring and informative. With time in hand post-retirement, I started writing a book on manufacturing management hoping it can be included in the curriculum for the management students. Unfortunately, I lost the manuscript which was kept in soft form while I was managing my files. I lost my motivation and then had given up the task. After some considerable time, one of my colleagues published a book. This triggered me to write the book again. Instead of my earlier decision to write a book on manufacturing management, I decided to narrate my career chronologically along with the learnings I picked out of the experience.

Another intent to write this book was to give back to the industry the experience and knowledge I have gained over the course of my career. Therefore, I am offering pro bono consulting services for Micro Small and Medium enterprises (MSME).

In narrating my experiences, I have deliberately omitted names of organizations. Few views that are shared are my perceptions of the situation and I might have erred, but my intentions were only to bring out lessons from such an experience. I also tried to be as accurate as possible in technical matters but any errors thereof may kindly be excused.

V. Murali
Mobile: +91 7042333280
Email: Lnswamy60@gmail.com

INTRODUCTION

I hail form a small township, Krishnagiri (now a district headquarters), where I did my schooling. I did my first two years of engineering from Government College of Engineering (GCE), Salem, followed by 3 years of specialization in Production Engineering from Government College of Technology (GCT), Coimbatore. Immediately after undergraduation, I pursued MBA from College of Engineering, Guindy (CEG), Chennai.

I dedicate my career success to my family who had to forgo stability because of my frequent changing of assignments and to all my colleagues for their whole-hearted support.

I started my career at the age of 24. I chose to become a Professional in Manufacturing Domain. My career progression has been listed as a table for the readers to comprehend my journey as with age comes experience. While I changed assignments at my whim and fancy mainly to avoid monotony in a particular assignment, the same brought accelerated career growth in turn.

Designation	Timeline	Industry	Product	Management style
Stores Officer	4 months	Light engineering	Aluminium cables and parts for Kitchen Appliances	Indian family-owned
Engineer – Planning	4 months	Graphite Processing	Electrodes	Indian Professional

Designation	Timeline	Industry	Product	Management style
Engineer – Planning & Industrial Engineering	4 months	Light Engineering	Agricultural Diesel Engines & Generators	Indian family-owned
Senior Industrial Engineer & System Analyst	2 years & 6 months	Light Engineering	Aluminium Extrusions	Indian family-owned
Assistant Manager – Vendor Development	2 years	Precision Optics & Light Engineering	Lens & Defence Equipment	Indian Professional
Assistant Works Manager	4 years	Light Engineering	Switchgears & Switchboards	Indian family-owned
Executive – Warehouse	2 years	Glass Processing	Float Glass & Mirrors	American MNC
Production Manager	3 years	Rubber Processing	Tyres	Indian Professional
General Manager – Operations	2 years	Ceramic Processing	Tiles	Indian family-owned
General Works Manager	3 years	Paint Processing	Paints	Indo-Japanese MNC
General Manager	3 years	Plastic Processing	Furniture, Crate & plastic parts for White Goods	Indian family-owned
Deputy General Manager	2 years	Heavy Engineering	Tyre Making Machinery	Indian MNC
Senior Deputy General Manager	2 years	Heavy Engineering	Tyre Making Machinery	Indian MNC

Designation	Timeline	Industry	Product	Management style
Joint General Manager	4 years	Heavy Engineering	Coal Pulveriser	Indo-Japanese Joint venture
Chief Executive	2 years & 6 months	Heavy Engineering	Axial Fans & Air Pre Heaters	Indo-Danish Joint venture
Vice President Manufacturing	2 years & 6 months	Light Engineering	Transmission Towers	Indian MNC

The purpose of writing this book is to showcase the practical aspects of Manufacturing Management drawn from my experience in various capacities in the industries I worked. I have shared my experience in each of the above assignments in individual chapters. I have given a title to each chapter in line with the most significant aspect of that assignment.

While I recommend the readers to read the book in the sequence it has been written, they may either choose to read any chapter which may interest them or the summary of lessons in various facets of management. In the summary of lessons, each lesson can be related to its significance by referring to the page number mentioned against the same.

The readers may find the first 3 chapters less interesting given that I spent only few months in each of these roles. While I have included them for the sake of completeness, my activities and derived insights from these roles were limited. Subsequent chapters offer a much larger length and breadth of concepts and lessons. The reader may also appreciate a shift from technical lessons at the early stages of the book to broader management lessons towards the later part of the book, which is a reflection of my growth in the management cadre. Hence, I urge the readers to continue reading till the end.

CHAPTER 1

IMPORTANCE OF STORES MANAGEMENT

"Ennithuniga karumam, thunindhapin ennuvam enbhadhu izhukku"
– Thirukkural

(Meaning: *Think well before acting; to act and then rethink is disgrace*)

Istarted my career in Stores as **Stores Officer** in a light engineering company. It was a small one with a total strength of around 60 people. This company was making Aluminium cables for transmission lines through an extrusion process as well as parts for Kitchen Appliances Industry using Low-Pressure Die Casting process. It was a sick unit under the BIFR (Banking Investment and Financial Reconstruction) Scheme. I did not know about this when I joined.

> *Do your groundwork before accepting an assignment.*

The Stores comprising Raw Materials, Finished Goods & Maintenance Spares, and Consumables was unorganized both in terms of physical storage as well as keeping records. It used to take significant time to locate the Spares & Consumables material. Even the lighting conditions were poor making it too difficult to look for the material. The materials were not classified in terms of value or use, and everything was kept in a mixed haphazard manner. There were no periodic inventory checks.

I started setting things right in terms of storage and record-keeping (refer to actions taken in the table below). I also ensured that the stock differences in physical and books were minimized by ensuring periodic stock-taking through perpetual inventory.

Experience in Stores gave me one profound learning, i.e., Stores is often a neglected function in most companies. Profit drain can happen in Stores due to poor management since, in most industries, raw material constitutes approximately two-thirds of the cost of the product.

The following lessons are not only from my above experience but captured from subsequent such experiences as well.

- *In a Stores Layout, it is a must to ensure "A place for everything & Everything in its place"*

- *Ensure a Perpetual Inventory system and reconcile stock differences immediately*

- *Ensure First in First Out (FIFO) for items with a shelf life*

- *Carry out an aging analysis for non-moving and slow-moving items and take timely decisions on disposal*

- *During disposal, do not wait to get a good price for the scrap, and in the process, waste your valuable storage space and run into an additional danger of good items getting mixed up with scrap and getting sold as scrap (This is how scrap dealers make good money). The faster we dispose of it, the better we are*

- *Whenever a new greenfield project is set up, ensure that Stores is up and running from the first day since this will be of great help in accounting for project materials and helps in completing the project on time by ensuring material availability*

CHAPTER 2

PLANNING AS A KEY MANAGEMENT FUNCTION

"Tough times never last; tough people do"
– Robert H Schuller

I joined as **Engineer - Planning** in a company making graphite electrodes (carbon) from small sizes to massive sizes. The electrodes are used in electric arc furnaces used for various applications.

The Planning Head (my boss) at that time was an old-timer who joined as a stenographer and had grown to occupy the current position in Planning. The Production Manager was not very comfortable with a non-professional handling this important function and hence my recruitment. I was recruited by the Production Manager with a clear intention of replacing him to run the department professionally. Unfortunately for me, he mentioned the same to my boss on my joining saying clearly that he should train me to subsequently replace him. This made my job difficult from day one. He allocated menial jobs to me and insulted me in front of the other staff whenever I asked for any clarification. I tolerated the same since I was learning the process.

Patience is a virtue through which you can win many battles.

The Manufacturing Process

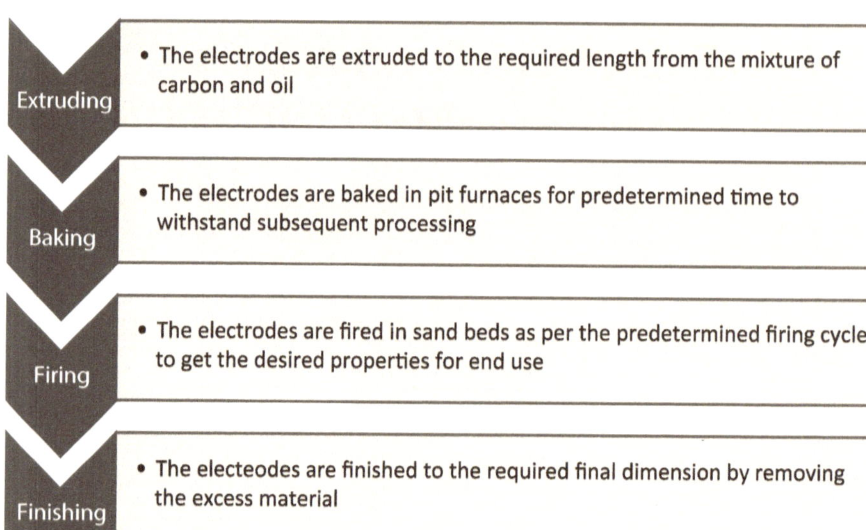

The main constraint in the whole production process was Firing since it consumes more power affecting Maximum Demand (MD). We needed to ensure the scheduling of simultaneous production of various batches in the Firing section that would result in MD not exceeding the limit sanctioned by the local electricity board authorities. Exceeding MD would result in payment of penalty initially and subsequent withdrawal of power sanction. Planning this stage was very tricky and challenging.

The company was using a manual Kardex system (Personal computers were not very popular in those days). It was my job to get the same filled with the production quantity of each product in various stages of manufacturing from the production reports. This results in Work in Progress (WIP) inventory in each stage. This Kardex system with the WIP data was the basis for planning production in various processes. This assignment taught me the intricacies of scheduling based on process lead time in a batch process industry.

Lessons from the above as well as in my subsequent assignments are listed below:

- *Planning is the sole agency responsible for delivering on time*
- *Planning is also responsible for gathering information internally & externally affecting delivery*
- *Know about each of the processes/facilities related to capacity and process time*
- *Plan for the bottleneck process/facility and subordinate everything else to the same*
- *Plan for buffer capacity in the upstream process to take care of rush orders, quality rejection, etc.*
- *Ensure staffing/automation in the finishing process for timely availability of the product for despatch without creating backlogs*

CHAPTER 3

IMPROVEMENTS THROUGH INDUSTRIAL ENGINEERING

"Those who dare to fail miserably can achieve greatly"
– John F Kennedy

My career continued as **Engineer – Planning & Industrial Engineering** in an Agricultural Diesel Engine & Diesel Generator manufacturing facility catering mainly to the agricultural industry. The factory consists of a Foundry with a Cupola furnace, Machine shop, and Assembly & Testing sections. It was manufacturing all critical parts in its facility while buying the balance parts from vendors.

I was asked to focus on Industrial Engineering studies for improvement and was given the freedom to choose my assignments. I had chosen the following.

Consumption Audit

The rationale for choosing this assignment was due to my observation of the melting process during a walk-through at the Cupola furnace. While charging the raw materials (pig iron and limestone), the contract labourer was charging the same in headloads. They stopped when the Cupola was full visually based on subjective judgement. The quantity of charge varied for every charge and the shocking observation was that there was no weighing scale available near the process.

I did a simple exercise of counting the number of headloads going into each charge for various crews and shifts. When I plotted these in a graph, the variances were as high as 10% resulting in both overcharging and undercharging. While overcharging increases the raw material cost (excess material resulting in excess slag), undercharging results in underutilizing the capacity of the furnace. I concluded that installing a weighing scale near Cupola to standardize the input would result in a savings of approximately Rs. 1.5 lakhs in a month (This was way back in 1985 and the savings were considered quite significant). My recommendation was accepted and implemented immediately.

> *Objective measurement is always better than subjective judgement.*

SFC Improvement using Statistical Tools

Improving SFC (Specific Fuel Consumption) which is a Unique Selling Proposition of their engine would gain market share for the company. SFC is dependent on the input setting of various parameters in their diesel engines and hence this was the next assignment I undertook. I had taken this assignment along with the Research & Development (R&D) Head who was instrumental in collecting the necessary data.

We needed to measure the specific fuel consumption (SFC) for various combinations of engine setting parameters and establish a relationship between the same. My R&D colleague collected all data regarding the above and I used a statistical regression model to arrive at the effect of various parameters on SFC. After many such exercises, when the regression coefficient (a statistical marker) was closer to 1, we froze those parameters and conducted repetitive tests on the engine with the frozen engine parameters and we could get a consistent better SFC.

> *Use Quantitative methods using mathematical/statistical models to be more objective.*

While the first assignment was appreciated by the management for the cost-saving it achieved, the second assignment was more gratifying when my R&D colleague presented a paper on the same in one of the automobile conferences, and the same was appreciated by the automobile community.

Lessons from the above, as well as my subsequent experiences, are listed below:

- *There are always opportunities available for improvement in every process*
- *To be an effective industrial engineer, you need to be observant and analytical*
- *Do not be afraid of failures as every failure is a step in the learning curve*
- *Be passionate to defend your work in front of adversaries*
- *Do not lose hope when your conclusion of a study and recommendation thereof is not accepted for implementation*

CHAPTER 4

PROCESS OPTIMIZATION THROUGH COMPUTERIZATION

"Twenty years from now, you will be more disappointed by the things you didn't do than the ones you did do"
– Mark Twain

My next employment was as **Senior Industrial Engineer** in an aluminium extrusion company making architectural, industrial, and commercial sections. It has a tool room to make the necessary extrusion dies using some of the latest state-of-the-art machines including an EDM (Electron Discharge Machine).

The Manufacturing Process

Casting
- The Casting of Billets from aluminium ingots of various grades depending on the end use is processed in a foundry

Extruding
- Extruding these casted billets is done in an Extrusion Press to extrude the required product sections to a length of 100 plus feet

Cooling
- Cooling of these extruded sections is done through transferring in an air cooling cum material handling system called Walking Beam (under installation) to a cutting machine

Cutting
- Cutting these cooled sections in a cutting machine into lengths specified by the customer and then bundled for onward storage & dispatch

In my first year, I handled assignments such as:

1) Manpower rationalization in the extrusion line with the installation of a walking beam thereby saving manpower. The exercise was done using **man-machine charts** from the process of extrusion to cutting. This captures the time taken to complete the task for various combinations of manpower used in the line. The optimum combination of manpower and time taken is chosen and the corresponding manpower is frozen.

2) Earlier there was no standard time for making dies which led to unpredictability of availability of dies, and this had resulted in the frequent stoppage of the extrusion line. I had fixed the standard times for their new dies in the Tool & Die making shop by doing a **Time study** for a few of their dies and extrapolated the data for their future ones. This enabled better planning resulting in the supply of dies to the extrusion line on time.

3) Stores was not able to measure the exact quantity of furnace oil received due to the elliptical shape of the container. I designed a calibration chart using a mathematical formula to measure the exact amount of fuel in the elliptical storage tank thus enabling them to account for receipts and stock more accurately.

> *Usage of modern management tools like Time Study etc. helps to improve the efficiency of operations.*

Computerization of Production Planning

During the 80s in the late 20th century, computers were still new. Unlike today's digital age where the world is only a click away, the use of computers in most industries was premature, including the manufacturing sector.

Considering my earlier experience in Planning, I was given the humungous responsibility of computerizing the company's planning operation. I was given an engineer to assist me in industrial engineering studies. I took up the computerization assignment as a challenge since I needed to do everything from scratch including my own knowledge of computerisation.

To facilitate the same, I was sent to a training program for 6 weeks in "Structured System Development at NIIT (National Institute of Information Technology). Equipped with the required skillsets, from being an Industrial Engineer, I became a **System Analyst**. I was reporting functionally to the Systems Manager in our corporate office while administratively reporting locally to the Head of the Unit. This had made my job more challenging as satisfying two bosses at crossroads is a tough one.

My job initially was to capture the planning process into logical diagrams. These diagrams show the input, the process, and the output for every step in the planning process for various stages of manufacturing such as:

a) Order input,

b) Splitting the Order Quantity into Production lots,

c) Releasing Production Order for each lot,

d) Releasing Requisition for Billets with grade and quantity along with intimation for ensuring the readiness of extrusion dies,

e) Scheduling Production Orders in Extruding section,

f) Recording actual production against each Production Order along with process details such as pressure, temperature, processing time, etc,

g) Recording stoppage of the line due to quality issues, breakdown, and extrusion die trials,

h) Rescheduling incomplete Production Orders,

i)   Follow the above steps till the whole order is completed,

j)   Generating various Management Information System reports.

In the process, some redundancies and duplication of processes were identified.

> ***Look into improvement in each of the current processes for removing redundancy***

The production team needed to be convinced to eliminate such redundancies. This initiative was partly successful. It was also a challenge to eliminate certain prevailing formats and bring in new formats with due acceptance from the production team.

> - ***Educate the stakeholders from end to end and make them process owners for their respective processes***
> - ***Simplify the formats for data collection and design them in consultation with the respective process owner for easy implementation***

I was given help in the form of programmers both in-house as well as from an external agency. They were tasked to write computer programs in line with the logic diagrams I have prepared for each step in the process. It took almost 1 ½ years to establish the desired system. We then did a test run in isolation and debugged the issues faced.

Subsequently, we ran the computerized system in parallel to the existing manual system. We further unearthed plenty of bugs as well as certain practical difficulties in executing this system. These were addressed. We also faced plenty of hiccups in getting accurate data inputs, but we managed to overcome them one by one. The main challenge was to convince the production team. They were hesitant to come out of their comfort zones of a well-established existing system, to accept Computerization. Gradually, they also accepted when they realized the benefits of a computerized system, one such benefit being the ready availability of information to make operational decisions.

> *It takes time to establish a new culture and we need to be resilient in launching a new initiative.*

Further lessons from the above are listed below which are applicable even for the current implementation of ERP (Enterprise Resources Planning) systems:

- *Make a cross-functional team comprising of representatives from various Operations to facilitate effective coordination and thereby successful implementation of a multi-stakeholder initiative such as Computerization*
- *Identify siloed shop floor practices and institutionalize them if appropriate*
- *Do not wait to achieve 100% perfection for implementation*
- *Implement the system in stages in the logical chain of events from beginning to end and keep integrating the new process*
- *Keep a subject matter expert to address bugs during the parallel run of existing and new systems*

CHAPTER 5

CHALLENGES IN VENDOR DEVELOPMENT

"The only way to achieve the impossible is to believe it is possible"
– Charles Kingsleigh

My next assignment was in a precision optics & light engineering company as **Senior Engineer - Planning**. The company is a 100% Export Oriented Unit. It manufactures precision optics and optical assemblies (lens for cameras and other optical devices) that get exported. It also manufactures optomechanical and optoelectronic assemblies for Indian Defence as deemed export.

The Manufacturing Process

Grinding
- Imported glass blanks fixed in a special tool are ground in tailor-made grinding machines to get a profile closer to the final one

Polishing
- The ground blanks are polished in polishing machines to get the final profile

Coating
- The polished blanks are coated with a chemical to get the necessary reflection parameters in a very sensitive imported equipment

Assembly & Packing
- The coated lenses would get packed either as loose pieces or assembled with a metal housing and packed in soft tissue papers and subsequently in cartons

Challenges in Coating

Some lenses must be coated multiple times to get the desired reflection parameters. This coating process was to be done in a clean environment to avoid foreign particles which would endanger the coating quality. The staff who are entering this area must wear cleanroom gowns and go through an air shower. This coating process had brought us lots of sleepless nights since any failure in this process would get the lenses rejected. We then would have to take a fresh batch and start the process all over again. This would derail the dispatch schedule and we had many such nervous moments. We had to plan such challenging coating products with enough cushion in lead time to meet delivery commitments.

Non-Optic Operations

Our facility included a machine shop, an anodizing plant, and an assembly shop. In the machine shop, few of the metallic parts for housing the lenses as well as for the defense equipment are made. In the anodizing plant, surface treatment on the metallic parts was done. In the assembly shop, assembling the defense equipment was done. Most of the parts for the defense equipment are developed through vendors. Vendor development was a highly challenging activity in this case as a) order quantity for defense equipment was small and vendors often looked-for high-volume orders and b) quality criteria for defense equipment are very stringent and so we needed to ensure we did our due diligence in selecting vendors to meet the required quality standards.

Challenges in Defense Orders

Every defense order would require a first piece inspection by a defense inspector for approval towards bulk production who was stationed with us full time. There used to be tight timelines for the first piece as well as the bulk supplies delivery. Among the defense equipment, we were also making night vision devices. These night vision devices must be checked on a new moon day in utter darkness in an external environment in front of the defense inspector. We would need to ensure the readiness of such night vision assemblies by the scheduled new moon day; else we would need to wait for a month to get the next opportunity to inspect. This would also result in delayed delivery with penalties. Hence, ensuring timely execution was a key responsibility of the planning section and the buck starts and stops at planning.

I was responsible for scheduling production in all the above sections to ensure delivery as per contract. Fortunately, I was given a Planning Assistant who was very energetic, supportive and contributing.

Vendor Development

After some considerable time in the above assignment, my colleague in vendor development resigned for better career prospects and I was transferred to this role.

Vendor development involved sourcing vendors for various metallic and non-metallic parts required for a variety of defense equipment. The challenges were two-fold. One was the low order quantity by defense along with stringent quality requirements. Additionally, we needed to develop the parts for the equipment within a short lead time due to the tight delivery requirements of defense. The other challenge was our company policy of not paying any advance to any vendor towards the development of tools required to manufacture the part wherever the same is needed. My colleague who had left created a very strong base of vendors, but new requirements kept coming up due to new orders. This was an exciting job, involving traveling across the country in search of vendors for components as crazy as camel hair for brushes, ivory for scales, etc.

Vendor Development Team

In the vendor development team, I had a team of 3 engineers and a stenographer. The tour for the team of engineers used to be planned in an ad hoc fashion resulting in last-minute travel involving unreserved bus journeys. We used to travel during the night and work during the day when we were on overnight journeys and travel during the weekend and work during the week when we were on long duration journeys. This was taking a toll on the team members' health. I put a stop to this practice and introduced a weekly schedule for each of the engineers so that bookings were done in train for sleeper berths. This helped them to do their job more healthily and hence motivated the team to a great extent.

I also started the practice of month-end lunch followed by a movie with all the team members at our own cost, and this activity significantly helped us bond both professionally and personally.

> - ***Take care of the team members and they will take care of the work without any micromanagement***
> - ***Informal get-together improves team building***

Gaining Vendor's trust

Generally, we used to pay our vendors on time. On one occasion, we faced a financial crunch and were short of working capital. Our finance head had warned us about the likely delay in payments to vendors. I immediately visited most of the vendors and forewarned them about the same. Barring a couple of vendors, most of them appreciated my informing them prior hand rather than facing the situation suddenly. It had given them enough time to manage their working capital accordingly.

> • *Always treat a vendor as a partner in your transaction with him*
> • *Be transparent with the vendor about any critical issues/situations. It would bring in trust in the long term*

Locating a Ghost Vendor with no Name & Address

While on a tour to Bangalore, I got a call from our MD informing me that a critical component for a defense equipment was missing. This was supplied by the defense itself for the paucity of time required for the development of the component. We were running short of time to submit the first piece for inspection. This component was a thin-walled casting to be made in the Investment Casting process. The vendor for the component was yet to be identified. Developing a vendor for the component would take considerable time due to the time taken for tool development. We knew our competitor had already developed a vendor for this component in Bangalore, but we knew neither the name nor the address. I was given the task of locating this vendor and getting a sample component. I was visiting area after area, street after street in Bangalore to locate this vendor with the only idea of the Investment Casting Process required for developing this component and I hit the bull's eye on the 3rd day in locating the vendor.

Getting him to agree to give us a sample component developed by our competitor was another challenge, but, in the end, we got the same and we could submit the first piece sample to defense on time. We also got a new vendor for our future requirements.

> *Every crisis always brings its own share of opportunities*

Neglecting Family

In this company, due to the freedom given to employees, all of us were very much involved in our work with lot of passion. The involvement was so much so that on one occasion, I had to miss the first tonsuring of my son due to an important customer visit. My son taunts me even now about how I gave primary importance to work and secondary importance to family.

> *Be with family on important occasions. It is going to be family that will be with you till the end and not the job.*

Some more lessons from the above stint as well from subsequent experiences are listed below:

- *Guide vendors on how to reduce their costs through better quality and waste reduction*

- *Always listen to them for any suggestions in the parts to be made and have the tenacity to take them up with your design section*

- *Have one primary vendor with a major share and one secondary vendor with a minor share for any high-volume requirement to tackle any crisis*

- *Correct the vendor upfront for any unrealistic price. This would avoid price revision and supply issues in future*

CHAPTER 6

INCREASING PRODUCTION THROUGH PRODUCTION MANAGEMENT

"The leader is one who, out of the clutter, brings simplicity ... out of discord, harmony ... and out of difficulty, opportunity"
– Albert Einstein

I joined as **Senior Engineer - Planning & Materials** in a switchgear manufacturing company that was headed by a retired Executive Director of BHEL (Bharat Heavy Electricals Ltd). The setup was a light engineering industry involving fabrication, machine shop, surface treatment, tool-room, switchgear assembly, and switchboard assembly.

The company was supplying HT and LT panel distribution boards to customers like State Electricity Boards as well as to various industries. It was also supplying HT switchgear such as Minimum Oil Circuit Breakers (MOCB), Vacuum Circuit Breakers (VCB), etc, and LT switchgear such as Air Circuit Breakers (ACB), Oil Circuit Breakers (OCB), and Fuse Switches (FSW) as stand-alone products. While the panel distribution boards involved fabrication that was done 100% in-house, the switch gears consisted of fabricated components as well as machined ones from castings and forgings. Some of the components were machined in-house and the balance were bought out.

Kitting for Assembly

The Bill of Material (BOM) was used manually to arrive at the requirement of components for each assembly and it was a very tedious task. We used cyclostyled copies of material of the BOM for the above exercise. For every assembly, the planning assistant had to go to Stores, check the physical availability of material against the BOM to arrive at the net requirement for each assembly, and plan for the manufacture of the balance. Any mistake in the above manual exercise resulted in a shortage of components for assembly and hence assembly was never executed on time. By design, the above exercise created issues for components that are drawn from stores after the shortage list is made. It also created issues for common components between assemblies when calculating the total requirement for such components.

I instituted a system of withdrawing such components physically for each assembly as a kit using the BOM. This helped in creating a shortage list for components not available against each assembly which was used for further planning. The above kitting exercise solved the problem of last-minute surprise shortages to a great extent.

Vendor Challenges

The company was not doing very well financially, and my boss was trying to restore its financial condition to a manageable level. Once I joined, many of the old vendors started pestering me for their payments overdue when I contacted them for fresh supplies. I had to convince them to continue to supply us. I committed to them that a percentage of their overdue payments would be settled along with every bill for the fresh supplies made (This was proposed by the accounts head when I approached him for clearing old dues). It was a tough job to convince those vendors to continue to supply to us against our requirements as well as to enable them to get their overdue payments which were a win-win for both. Most of them agreed, and we were able to slowly settle their old dues and make new payments as well. For those who did not agree, we needed to develop new vendors for the regular supply of components and my past network of vendors helped me a great deal.

> *Vendors are loyal to you if you ensure their payments are on time.*

Interaction with Section Heads

As a planning engineer, I started spending my time in the shop and started interacting with all production section heads. I wanted to have first-hand knowledge of the issues that affect production and hence delivery. Thanks to the one-on-one interactions, section heads started becoming closer to me in opening out their issues. They were all very much afraid of my boss who used to shout at them and scold them. But he used to tell me often that "Shouting is not good management" which I failed to follow till the end of my career due to my short temper (I missed a promotion in one of my subsequent assignments because of the above). The section heads started using me to communicate some of their genuine production issues to my boss. I raised these issues with my boss when he was in a good mood and was successful in resolving most of them.

- *Relationship building helps you to get problems resolved in the organization*
- *If you do not address your weakness when you are young enough, your career would suffer when it mattered*

Promotion

After 9 months of my joining, I was promoted as Assistant Works Manager (AWM) in charge of total production and maintenance. When I tried to express my surprise cum shock over this promotion due to my lack of experience in production, I was assured by my boss that my hard work and initiative would take care of the lack of experience, and he had every confidence in me that I would do well. Had it not been for that moment, I would have probably ended up as either a planning head or a materials head but never a manufacturing professional.

> *Opportunity knocks at your door when least expected. Grab it with both hands.*

Due to my good relationship with all section heads, I was readily accepted as their boss which made my job easier to perform.

Quality of food in the canteen

The first issue I faced after I got promoted to AWM is about the differential quality of food served in the workmen's canteen as compared to the executive canteen. To resolve this, I started having lunch in the workmen's canteen, and suddenly, the complaints vanished. I didn't know whether it was due to improvement in quality after I started eating there or otherwise, but this incident had brought me closer to the workmen as I had treated them as equals in sharing the same food and eating in the same canteen. Since then, I started having food in both the canteens alternatively. This enabled me to resolve issues with quality, engineering, accounts, and other teams over an informal chat during lunch in the executive canteen, and at the same time, kept my ears to the ground for workmen issues before they become critical in the workmen canteen.

> • *Solving sensitive problems needs a plunge into it directly without resorting to delegation*
> • *Use informal channels for identifying and resolving issues*

I started working on the various prevailing issues of manufacturing. The issues were multifold such as low productivity in fabrication, timely availability of machined components for assembly, interdepartmental squabbling, errors in drawing, etc.

Challenge of low productivity in Fabrication

In the fabrication shop, we were making switchboard panels with the necessary brackets for fixing various elements of the switchgear assembly as well as a few sheet metal components for switchgear. We had hydraulic and mechanical presses for making frames for the panels and components. Fabrication of the switchboard panels was done in sets of 2 workstations, namely, setting and welding. In the setting workstation, parts of the various panels were tack welded as per drawing and handed over to the welding workstation for full welding.

I found that the reason for low productivity in fabrication is a lack of traceability of required components. This was mainly due to poor housekeeping. All the components including old unused ones were kept haphazardly. Most of the production time was lost due to the time required in tracing the required components for the setting. This led to not only the idleness of the setting workstation but also led the idleness of the corresponding welding workstation due to the irregular supply of set panels for full welding.

Myself along with my fabrication team comprising 2 young engineers had started organizing components in front of each setting workstation for the next day's production after the shift hours were over (ours was a one-shift operation). We removed all old unused obsolete components keeping only the necessary components in an organized manner to enable easy identification. Since this unit was on the outskirts of the city with a very poor public transport facility, all the staff were provided with transport facilities by the company. Generally, overstay was discouraged because of this reason. My team and I didn't get bogged down with such inconveniences and we went home late only after ensuring material availability for the next day. (This involved walking half an hour and then waiting for public transport). We continued this practice till the production was stabilized and subsequently could do this exercise during the shift itself. This had doubled the fabrication output from the initial 0.4 MT (Metric Tonne) to 0.8 MT every day.

> *Certain solutions need additional efforts to bring an end to the problem.*

I had also called the fabrication workmen for a meeting in our conference room (which was never done earlier) and politely demanded that each of them increases their current production numbers by one. (This meant a 15% overall increase right away). They had raised many issues in the meeting including material availability and I patiently listened and agreed to resolve most of their issues. Ultimately, they agreed to my demand and started delivering their commitment the next day.

> *Make workmen your collaborators rather than your low-level subordinates and this would bring wonders.*

We also had a severe quality issue in terms of waviness in the HR (Hot Rolled) steel sheets and it took more time to fabricate. This also had reflected badly on the aesthetic aspect of the panels once they got painted. Despite our repetitive feedback to the supplier, they were not getting the problem rectified. I had decided to try a new supplier who had just then started business. Their products were far superior in quality, and surprisingly, we got the products at cheaper rates which was an added benefit.

> *Sometimes the solution to a problem rewards you with unexpected benefits*

All the above steps had increased the fabrication production to 1.1 MT per day from the initial 0.4 MT per day, and suddenly, we found our assembly was getting flooded with fabricated material. The fabrication workmen were happy that they were able to perform their work without any interruption. Overall, we also improved the housekeeping of the shop by removing unwanted things. This improved the visibility of the wanted material and yielded better results.

> *Good housekeeping always improves productivity*

Machine Shop Challenges

In the machine shop, manufacturing was done just to complete targets as per raw material (RM) availability without considering the requirements of assembly. I addressed this challenge by drawing a production plan for the machine shop based on the assembly plan and asking the machine shop to strictly adhere to the same. I had also ensured RM availability for the plan by arranging them and ensured only the required RM was getting issued for making components as per the production plan. This ensured that the assembly got their material in the order of priority they wanted. I should have done the above during my planning stint, but I was focusing more on feeding material to assembly daily by expediting vendors. I was relying more on my planning assistant to ensure material availability from the shops.

> *Delegating responsibilities may not get the desired results unless supervised*

Bought-out Components

Since I was already handling materials, ensuring the supply of bought-out components was relatively easier. I only had to ensure timely payments which I managed to get with the support of my boss.

I also started organizing regular interdepartmental meetings inside the company and informal gatherings outside the premises to bring in mutual understanding and teamwork, and this solved most of their internal squabbles.

> *The strength of an organization lies equally in its informal structure as the formal one*

Collaboration with Engineering

I managed to get timely intervention from engineering department for drawing related issues when I changed the culture from blaming through precipitation of issues to resolving issues with them. I organized regular meetings between production which included some workmen and the engineering team, and this brought down the errors in drawings to a great extent. Engineers from the engineering section started spending a considerable amount of time in shops on their own (which earlier was happening only on demand and resulting in more conflicts) to improve drawings, and this was a welcome change.

> *Collaboration can help solve issues when used tactfully while blame game spoils relationships*

The ultimate beneficiary was not only the business getting increased revenue from timely deliveries but also the workmen who had started getting better production incentives due to the above. I became acceptable to all employees including workmen and they started listening to me for any new changes I wanted to bring in.

Debottlenecking in Fabrication

I wanted to increase our capacity in fabrication as this was becoming a bottleneck for us. When I analysed the process, I found that the workstation involving setup beds for panels (a metal platform on which numerous holes are drilled and tapped for holding frames of the various sizes of panels for tack welding) was the main constraint. I had a fabrication worker who was about to retire and using that as an excuse, he was not contributing to the production efforts. I had a long discussion with him, and I offered him to take up the job of making a new setup bed which involved considerable skill in designing and making the same. He talked again about his post-retirement life. I told him that if he contributes to this effort, I shall certainly address his grievance and look into possibilities of helping him. He trusted me and we got a new setup bed made which resulted in increased fabrication output.

Retired worker as a vendor

After consultation with my boss regarding helping this worker after his retirement, I asked him to set up a small fabrication facility with minimum investment. I loaded him regularly with the fabrication of a particular set of panels which was not very productive to fabricate in our shop. The above incident had ensured his livelihood and increased my credibility among the workmen that I was a man of words and would always take care of them.

> *Make sure to live up to your commitments to increase your credibility*

I had also participated in almost all family functions of my workmen and other team members, and gradually, I developed good relationships with almost everybody on the shop floor. There were moments I lost my cool with few of the workmen on the shop floor, but I was surprised about the support received from other workmen during such instances.

> *Informal relationships help diffuse many crises, and this is what is called as Managing Through Influence in the business world*

Challenge of Effluent Treatment Plant

We faced the issue of the effluent treatment of chemicals from our surface treatment plant. The pollution control board has warned us repeatedly of dire consequences if we don't treat them. I had a transparent discussion with the pollution control engineer who had visited us. I explained to him about the financial difficulties we were facing and how we could not afford an ETP at that point and sought his help as to how to manage the issue within the framework of the law. He helped us with a simple solution that was cost-effective and at the same time was conforming to the rules.

> • *Sometimes the solution lies with the person who raises the problem*
> • *Asking for help (which many hesitate to do) helps*

Bonus Negotiation

During the bonus negotiations with the union, I experienced something unbelievable. My boss and I entered the conference room where the union representatives were waiting. The president of the union wanted to present his demand, but my boss stopped him. He told them that he empathized with them (It was a good year for the company financially after a long time and workmen had not gotten a reasonably good bonus for a long time) for their past poor financial rewards and would not like to hassle regarding bonus negotiation. He had a final figure that he felt was reasonable and fair. If the union had felt otherwise, it would be their choice to walk out and stretch the discussion for long. The union president asked for the figure. When my boss revealed the figure, the union representatives were dumbfounded as they never expected such a high figure and they gladly agreed.

They wanted to end the meeting then and there to inform the workmen. My boss insisted they spend more time in the conference room along with him. He was saying that let other people outside think that we were seriously negotiating while we were discussing normal day-to-day issues like inflation, local politics, etc. While the bonus settlement took only the first 10 min, the balance of 50 min was spent on casual and loose talk. Subsequently, all the workmen were very happy to receive the bonus. I had never heard of such a fast bonus settlement in my career.

Later my boss told me that he would want peace on the shop floor as we were turning around our business just then. He also wanted me to focus on more productive work rather than attending to union hassles. Ultimately, he said that the workmen also deserve better, and it is only fair they share in our good fortune.

> ***Fair treatment of unionized workmen always brings peace and harmony in the long term***

CHAPTER 7

NUANCES OF SHIFT MANAGEMENT

"Life is ten percent what happens to you and ninety percent how you respond to it"
– Charles Swindoll

My next assignment was in an American multinational company making float glass for the first time in India for architectural and automotive applications. I joined as **Executive - Warehouse**, managing packing & warehousing in shifts.

The Manufacturing process involves:

Hot End Production

a) Melting silica sand along with lime, soda, and cutlets (broken glass) at around 1600 degrees centigrade,

b) The molten glass is maintained at approx. 1200 degrees centigrade to achieve homogeneous specific gravity,

c) The molten glass is fed into a tin bath at a temperature of 1100 degrees centigrade where molten tin is kept under positive pressure to avoid oxidation. The glass flows on the tin surface forming a floating ribbon (hence the name **float glass**) with a perfectly smooth surface on both sides and of even thickness. As the glass flows on the tin bath, the temperature is gradually reduced from 1100 degrees to 600 degrees centigrade,

d) The glass ribbon at the above temperature is pulled off the bath by rollers at a controlled speed. Once off the tin bath, the glass sheet is passed through a kiln for approximately 100 meters. This cools the glass gradually to enable annealing without strain and ensures it does not crack due to the temperature change.

Lower Line Production

a) The speed of the rollers decides the thickness of the glass. Higher speed results in lower thickness and lower speed in higher thickness. The thickness was ranging from 2 mm to 32 mm based on the end application. Once the desired thickness of the glass is achieved, the glass was cut to the required dimensions of width and length, using diamond cutters set on the conveyor line.

b) Smaller-sized glass is lifted off the conveyor line manually for packing while vacuum cups are used for bigger-sized glass. The glass is packed in open wooden boxes which were glued with thermocol. These open wooden boxes were kept on a movable trolley adjacent to the conveyor.

Warehousing

a) Empty wooden boxes were brought from the storage yard and prepared for packing by gluing thermocol on the box as well as on the lids,

b) The trolleys with the open empty box were supplied to both sides of the conveyor line by forklifts. The lids glued with the thermocol were retained by the packing personnel. On their return trip, the forklift brought back the trolley with glass filled boxes,

c) The filled boxes were closed with lids using nails in the packing area. A pneumatic gun is used for hammering the nails at a faster pace to improve productivity,

d) The packed boxes were bundled based on the glass thickness. They are moved to the available spaces in the warehouse area and then stacked one below the other or kept one behind the other depending upon the size. Both the bundling and moving to the warehouse area were done using forklifts.

Bringing the empty wooden boxes and preparing them was being performed by contract workmen. All the other operations were performed by permanent workmen called technicians.

Shift Operations

All the shift staff would come 15 min earlier at the beginning of the shift and take over the operations from the earlier shift personnel in their respective functions. In the warehouse, we needed to check the working condition of the line. This includes sufficient box availability in the line, availability of empty boxes, empty trolleys, and proper working conditions of the forklifts & nail guns. The understanding was that the outgoing shift should ensure minimum availability of all the above resources for a minimum of 15 min of uninterrupted operations in the subsequent shift.

> *Look at your next shift operation as an internal customer and ensure a smooth handover*

The challenge in the above assessment is the timely supply of boxes to the Lower Line failing which the unpacked glass would be kept in racks (padded with rubber) that are limited in number. If the racks were not available, the glass would get crushed in the crusher at the end of the line. These are losses of production for the shift crew. All hell would break loose, and the shift Warehouse Executive would be nothing short of crucified by the Lower Line Executive and the Shift Manager. There was heavy competition among the different shift crews for the best production performance. The problem occurred mostly during the running of thin glasses. This came off the line very fast and hence needed quick replenishment of boxes. Usually, 50% of the earlier shift crew technicians were retained on overtime to cope with the packing load in such thin glass runs.

The reasons for the above situation were mainly the breakdown of forklifts and pneumatic guns. Due to continuous production, the above equipment was hardly available for any preventive maintenance resulting in these breakdowns. Every shift executive would try to keep spare nail guns but in vain because of the excessive usage of the same.

> *Never release all available resources at the same point in time. Ration critical resources*

The glasses are produced in ascending or descending order of thickness. It was unfortunate for me that I started the job when the thin glass had started running. The demand for boxes was high during this time. I was struggling to cope with the pressure of supply of boxes to the line with the added issues of breakdown in forklifts, nail guns, etc. I got frequently hammered by our Lower Line Executive and Shift Manager during my initial days.

Working in the shifts itself was new to me and added to that was the pressure due to the nature of the job. We were also woken up during the day after completing a night shift to clarify any issues that occurred in our shift affecting the subsequent shift (Like glasses found broken in the warehouse affecting dispatch). Overall, the job was physically and mentally exhausting and overwhelming.

Untimely food and sleep were taking their toll on my health during the adjustment period.

> *Have a healthy diet to work through various time zones in various shifts*

Patience and perseverance teach lots of things and soon I started understanding the nuances of the job and started performing. One of the nights, I went to the extent of breaking into a shelf belonging to the mirroring section which works only during the day shift to get nail guns to keep my shift running. Even though I was warned not to repeat such things in the future by our Managing Director the next day, I could see the admiration in his eyes as to how far I was stretching to discharge my responsibility.

> *Any shift engineer deciding on the shift has taken the right decision irrespective of others questioning the decision later based on hindsight*

Deputation to the USA

Although I was on the technical front, recognizing my qualification in management, and in appreciation of my continuing good performance, I was sent to our company's headquarters in USA for a conference in ABC (Activity Based Costing) along with an accountant. This was a great opportunity that few get in their early careers in those days, and I was fortunate to experience it.

> *Patience along with perseverance solves all problems, and rewards would follow performance sooner or later*

Lost Opportunity for Promotion

There used to be meetings between operators and management staff periodically. In one such meeting, I lost my cool and shouted at the operators for not understanding a point clarified by the management. This was noticed by the top management. At that time, I was being considered for promotion and my aggressive behaviour had cost me the promotion.

> ***Aggressive behaviour burns the bridges and never yields results or benefits.***

Safety, Health & Environment (SHE)

In this company, I learned how American management values life by the emphasis they place on SHE. The intolerance shown towards safety violations through disciplinary action was unbelievable. The amount of money spent on providing quality PPEs (Personal Protective Equipment) to all employees was exorbitant. Whenever the shop floor was littered with broken glass due to breakage, even the General Manager himself did not hesitate to pick a broom and sweep the floor because somebody could slip over the glass and hurt themselves. The top management was walking the talk by setting themselves as examples to the whole team.

Whenever any safety incident involving First Aid was reported, the Shift Manager took charge of the investigation. In case of any minor accident where the employee was sent home but resumed duty the next day, the General Manager took charge of the investigation. In case of any lost-time accident involving absenteeism for days to come, the MD himself took charge of the investigation. In all the above situations, the top management would make themselves available on the spot for investigation irrespective of the time of the day.

> *Safety starts at the TOP*

When there was flu in the adjoining city, preventive medicine was immediately imported and provided to all employees. The management took pride in ensuring a safe and healthy work environment, and I learned immensely in SHE to follow in my subsequent assignments.

> - *Emphasize human safety & health and don't take things lightly*
> - *A safe work environment is always rewarding in terms of the high morale in the organization*

PPC (Personal Positive Commitment)

This company has an excellent performance appraisal system wherein performance was recorded continuously through a document called PPC. In PPC, every employee and his supervisor record exemplary as well as poor performance on a day-to-day basis through mutual consent. This document is used at the end of the year for performance appraisal as the objective proof of performance.

> *Continuous assessment through recording of performance would lead to a fair and transparent performance appraisal process*

Chapter 8

CAPACITY ENHANCEMENT THROUGH DEBOTTLENECKING

"Let us never negotiate out of fear. But let us never fear to negotiate"
– John F Kennedy

Iwas hired in a reputed Tyre manufacturing unit as **Production Manager**. I was selected by this company to head production in a new unit which the company was planning to take over shortly. I had been assigned to one of their existing units to get inducted into the job and understand the operations and thereby prepare me to take over the new assignment. When I joined the unit, there was already a Production Manager who had been recently transferred from the parent unit. When I met him, he uttered the most sensible thing," As long as we do not discuss each other's salary, we can remain good colleagues" and I followed this principle till the end of my career.

> *Sensitive information affecting working relationships should never be shared among colleagues*

The Manufacturing Process

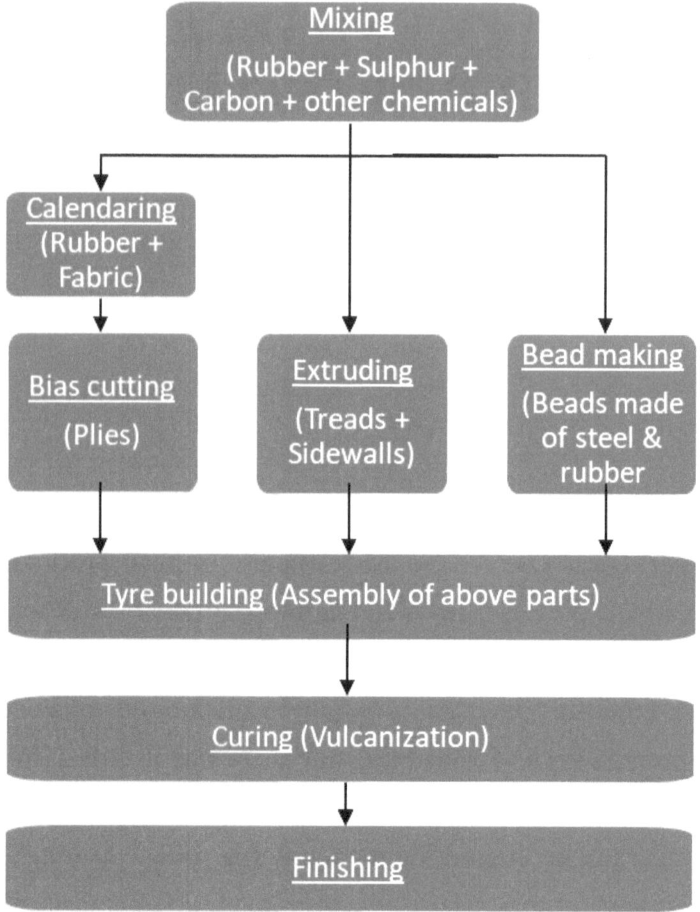

The Unit was making all types of tyres which included scooters, motorcycles, passenger vehicles, commercial vehicles such as trucks, and tractors (OTR or Off-The-Road tyres were made in our parent unit). The Unit was also making Radial tyres for passenger vehicles which was a separate section by itself. The output was measured in tonnage and the bigger tyres we made, higher was the tonnage.

Division of Responsibilities

My colleague explained to me that dividing the production sections between both of us would lead to disputes/conflicts. Since the manufacturing was done in batches, any problem in the upstream process would invariably affect the output in the downstream process. He also mentioned that there were always conflicts between Production Managers in the past with the ultimate detrimental effect on production output. He suggested that all the sections be handled jointly by both of us and that we divide responsibilities as follows: handling the production along with managing the union would be handled by him and improvements in terms of implementation of new systems, Manpower planning, Manpower rationalization, Budgeting, etc. would be handled by me. I decided to accept his suggestion for the following reasons:

1) He was very sincere when he explained the above,

2) In a new strong union environment, the above suggestion would help me to understand my job better and

3) I had to move out when the new unit is going to be taken over.

While my colleague was focusing on union and day-to-day production issues, I was focusing on system-related issues like proper data collection for analysis, budget, manpower requirements for various product mixes, etc. To be honest, I was acting more like a deputy than the man-in-charge. My colleague treated me with respect and regard, and he always kept me informed of any of his plans, but he always had an upper hand in production management because of his experience in the industry.

> *It is not qualifications alone but the experience that matters*

CLIP & CVP

In the meanwhile, management had brought McKinsey & Company as external consultants for improvements in the company; one of the improvement projects they undertook was the fulfilment of customer orders. Since the output was always measured in terms of tonnage, the tendency was towards allocating more resources towards heavy tyres like truck, tractor, and heavy passenger vehicle tyres. This had always led to lightweight tyres like scooters and motorcycles and other low-end passenger vehicle tyres getting step-motherly treatment. Hence, we never met the demand for these tyres. McKinsey introduced 2 measurement parameters called CLIP (Committed Line-Item Performance) and CVP (Committed Volume Performance). While CLIP would measure if all line items which are the SKUs (Stock Keeping Unit) are produced, CVP would measure if the volume requirements against each SKU are met to a minimum 95% level. These 2 metrics were being reviewed continuously by the top management. Now we were left with no choice but to focus on all tyres to meet the demand.

> *Do justice to your responsibilities in addressing all customers as each customer is important to the business*

While the CLIP & CVP metrics were achieved to the desired level now and met management expectations, we took a hit on tonnage. This was not acceptable to the management since the total budgeting exercise was based on tonnage.

Debottlenecking

We had an Executive Director (ED) who visited us regularly. This gentleman was an Industrial Engineer who ultimately became ED -

Manufacturing. He had an innate knack for asking all the right questions and I learned a lot from him. During his visit, he used to question us about the production issues including union, and in the process of questioning, guided us towards improvements.

> *Asking the right questions in a situation is one of the keys to problem-solving*

After having one such discussion with him regarding the low tonnage, my colleague and myself started looking into the process in detail to identify the bottleneck. We found the answer when we discussed the green tyre building production with the section-in-charge. We always calculated capacity in terms of the equipment we had. But interestingly, there was a human operation involved viz. the ply preparation/ply loading in these tyre building machines. This operation dictated the output of the machine and not the equipment capacity. The helper who does this job is called a ply-boy. Every ply-boy serves more than one machine depending upon the construction features of the tyre.

The job of the ply-boy demands skills to understand the variety of available plies which are very high in number. We found that our tyre building machines were underutilized compared to their capacity because we did not have sufficient trained ply boys.

My colleague immediately instructed that a certain number of helpers should be earmarked for this training and be trained with immediate effect. After we trained the first batch of ply-boys, our production started increasing and soon we started producing from the initial 70 MT per day to the targeted 100 MT per day continuously. This was a huge breakthrough for us, and it also taught us the value of human intervention in a man-machine equation for capacity planning.

> *Never forget the human factor in any capacity calculation*

I further took up the assignment of developing a macro in Microsoft Excel which gives section-wise manpower requirements on a shift-to-shift basis. This is based on the product mix we make in every shift, and the productivity norms agreed by the union. This tool was used by our shift superintendents to effectively use manpower in deploying trainee apprentices.

> *Be updated with modern tools and don't hesitate to put them to use for better management*

Union & Wage Settlement

In the meanwhile, wage settlement discussion had started, and this was a real eye-opener for me. I learned a lot from my colleague about how to handle negotiations with a union and how one should practice patience in such an exercise. We used to sit in discussions with the union for productivity negotiation from morning till midnight and wait for the other party to blink. We kept sticking to the same demands of productivity irrespective of the time, and we kept silent most of the time while allowing the union to put forth their demands. The union representatives would beg us to postpone the meeting after a tiresome day. However, we wouldn't agree saying that the union was not cooperative while we were ready to listen to them and continue discussion. All credit to my colleague who used this strategy to wear them out and bring them around to accepting our demands to a great extent if not 100%.

In any negotiation, patience is the key

Dealing with Work Stoppage

There were many occasions of work stoppage in the plant. Whenever there is a work stoppage, there is more than one way to deal with the situation. Normally, there would be an immediate reaction from the management as to why the work stoppage had happened, and the union are approached by the management. In most of such situations, because of the immediate reaction, the union gains the upper hand and ensures that their demands are met without any justification.

My colleague followed a different strategy of sitting out the work stoppage without approaching the union, thus transferring the pressure to the union, and making sure the union approached us to resolve the issue. Else the workmen would pressurize the union representative to resolve the issue, as otherwise, there was a possibility of their wage cut for the work stoppage. My colleague would always start the meeting with the demand that work should resume before starting the discussion and wages would be cut for the duration of work stoppage. This generally shifted the issue from their new demands to not cutting the wages, thereby diluting their demands. This strategy worked many times and the union had become very cautious about work stoppages for any unjustified reasons.

Always keep the other party guessing in a critical union situation

At this point, my colleague got promoted as Chief Production Manager to handle total production. The management transferred me to handle

Stores & Excise to avoid any misunderstanding and embarrassment between us. The takeover plan for the new unit didn't materialize, and hence my opportunity of going to the new unit was lost.

Stores & Excise

One of the first tasks I handled as Head of Stores & Excise was to dispose around 350 MT of scrap lying in our scrap yard for years. The previous incumbent did not want to handle the same because of the sensitivity of selling scrap (Most of the scrap dealers are notorious for taking good material along with scrap material through unscrupulous means due to which the deciding authority was always perceived to be corrupt). There were a lot of talks among staff and workmen about my decision to dispose, but I had the support of management, and they were willing to bet on my integrity.

> *Certain decisions need courage and conviction however unpopular the decision may be*

I also started addressing many old pending issues like show-cause notices issued by the excise department. I met the excise authorities regularly and provided all the data they wanted. I could resolve some of them but not all.

> *Do not live with old issues. Resolve them one way or another*

There used to be regular raids by the excise department on us to check the inventory of trailer tyres and light commercial vehicle tyres which are similar in size but different in composition. Since the duty component was low for trailer tyres due to end application in agricultural sector, the dealers used to buy trailer tyres but sell them as light commercial vehicle tyres. The excise department would think that the dealers were conniving with us in this issue and hence the frequent raids. We time and again proved that there was no issue at our end, and we could not control the dealers' transactions.

> ***If you are fair and transparent, there is nothing to be afraid of***

A new ED-Manufacturing had joined after a new MD took over the organization. The company had recently bought a small unit. The new ED transferred me to this small unit (which is in a different city) as Production Head. I considered it a demotion since the scope of work and responsibilities were not challenging due to the size of the unit. Hence, I declined to move and continued to work as Head - Stores & Excise.

> ***If you have confidence in yourself, you can always make a firm choice***

CHAPTER 9

PRODUCTIVE MAINTENANCE IN CONVEYOR LINE MANUFACTURING

"You can't be the bottleneck in decision making"
– Alexander Cartwright

I joined a ceramic tile manufacturing company as **General Manager-Operations.** The manufacturing facility was equipped with state-of-the-art equipment imported from Italy and was operating 24hours a day and 7 days a week. My responsibility included Production, Quality, Maintenance, Purchase, and Despatch.

Upon joining, our HR head told me that the Plant Head to whom I would be reporting and who takes care of product development did not trust anybody. It was going to be a challenge working along with him. The management hired me intending to relieve him of day-to-day operations and have him focus more on product development and cost reduction initiatives, etc. I was made to understand that the operating staff were typically apprehensive of taking decisions fearing his wrath and would wait for him to do so in many situations.

The Manufacturing Process

Slurry making
- Mixing of clay with water to make the Slurry

Spray drying
- The slurry is dried in a Spray Drier to get homogeneity in clay, resulting in the clay powder

Pressing
- The Clay powder is pressed into tiles using dies in a hydraulic press

Baking
- The tiles are baked in an oven to get the strength for withstanding further processing

Glazing
- The baked tiles are coated with glass slurry along with colouring agents that are seperately ground in ball mills

Screen printing
- Different colors are printed in the required pattern on the glazed tile through a screen

Firing
- The tiles are heated to a temperature of 1500 degrees centigrade to get the final product

Sorting
- The fired tiles are sorted into different grades based on defects online in an automated sorting machine along with the manual intervention

Packing
- The sorted tiles are packed online in carton boxes along with online printing (such as model, size, colour, quality grade, MRP, etc)

Strapping
- Each carton box is strapped online with plastic straps in an automatic strapping machine

Palletising
- The strapped carton boxes are stacked in a wooden pallet

Shrink wrapping
- The wooden pallet is shrink wrapped using a plastic film in a Shrink Wrapping Machine to avoid slippage and breakage of the tiles in the carton boxes

Right from Pressing to Firing, the tile is transported in a continuous conveyor line. From Firing furnace, the tiles were transported by a forklift to Sorting Machine. From Sorting to Strapping, a separate conveyor is used. Maintaining such a plant involving equipment imported from beginning to end was a challenging task.

> *In a conveyor line production setup, delegate all decisions to run the line continuously since line stoppage is a very costly affair*

Production Performance

We were producing only 80% of the capacity then, and our Managing Director was pushing us to achieve 100%. The gap between the actual production and the capacity was mainly due to line stoppages. These line stoppages were caused because of breakdown of various equipment. The line was also stopped due to quality issues when the colour/shade/design of the tiles produced differed with the approved colour/shade/design of the approved master tile kept by the quality section. Any simple quality deviation was to be approved by our Plant Head. Quality team personnel were afraid of making decisions because of Plant Head's nature, and the line would often be stopped waiting for him to give decision. During the back shifts beyond midnight or weekends, if there is a quality issue, a changeover for a simple glazed tile would be decided by the shift in-charge and run.

Spares

I started focusing on breakdowns, and I found that the lines were stopped for spares more often than attending the breakdown. In consultation with the maintenance head, I prepared a list of spares, got approval from the Plant Head, and got them airlifted. This brought down the downtime due to spares. We also started monitoring the spare stock to enable us to re-order in time for replenishment.

> *Spares Management is key to Maintenance Management*

Preventive Maintenance (PM)

Another reason for stopping the line was for preventive maintenance. I initiated the idea of doing PM in parts rather than for a whole line whenever the line was getting stopped for quality or model changeover. During a model changeover, the line is stopped many times to match the production with quality standards. The above arrangement of doing PM in parts ensured better line availability for production resulting in more capacity utilization.

> *A flexible approach leads to better solutions*

Quality Issues

As regards stoppage for quality, I was encouraging the quality team to take decisions much to the discomfort of the Plant Head. He indirectly fired me by firing the quality people in front of me whenever things went wrong due to certain poor decisions, but such incidents were less significant compared to the overall quality acceptance, and our lines were producing more.

I also deliberately planned for simple tiles with only top glaze or designs with single screen printing to be run whenever there is a change in the model during back shifts and weekends. This has also reduced the line stoppage to a great extent.

> *Encourage your staff to make decisions and support them to learn from their mistakes*

All the above efforts had resulted in capacity touching 100% and the top management including the Plant Head was happy. He started opening up and listening to me.

> *Results speak louder than words*

Cost Reduction through substitution – A Failure

We were using furnace oil for operating our Spray Drier. As part of the cost reduction measure, we had substituted a cheaper alternative fuel in place of furnace oil since the thermal properties of the alternative were better than furnace oil. To our disappointment, the spray drier stopped one day, and we found the fuel pump was not working. Fortunately, we had a spare fuel pump, and we could restart the furnace immediately. On further analysis, we found fuel pump was not working because of the chemical corrosion effect of the substituted fuel. We immediately shifted back to furnace oil. We did an exercise on the cost of more frequent replacement of fuel pumps which were imported vs the cost-saving in fuel and based on this analysis, we moved back to furnace oil permanently. A similar proposal to add fuel additives in DG (Diesel Generator) to reduce specific fuel consumption was turned down because the OEM (Original Equipment Manufacturer) was not comfortable with the additive being added.

> *Cost reduction through substitution should always be thoroughly deliberated before implementation*

In-house Subcontracting

We were buying wooden pallets for storing the boxes of tiles. The cost of transporting these pallets from our vendor's end was significant in the total landed cost of the pallet due to the high volume occupied by the pallet. I approached a new vendor and after committing to him a good volume of business, we started procuring timber required for making pallets. With this initiative, we started making pallets in our Plant itself by employing the vendor's workmen. This brought down the cost of transportation to one-third of its original cost and resulted in a significant savings in the total cost of the pallets which were being consumed in high volume.

> *In-house subcontracting is always cost-effective provided the necessary infrastructure is available*

Severe Accident

There was an accident where one of our maintenance personnel was gravely injured while attending to a breakdown and his leg had got cut and separated. We were in utter shock and distress seeing this mishap, but we ensured that the cut leg was kept immediately in an icebox. I took him to the nearest metro city in an ambulance after giving due first aid and admitted him to the hospital and handed over his cut leg in the icebox. A major operation was performed to restore his leg. I arranged for a helper from the factory to stay with him during the pre-operative and post-operative days who'd also help him during physiotherapy. I also ensured that he was visited by one of our staff every week to give him words of encouragement to keep his morale high. I was also visiting him once a month. We could save his leg due to the timely and best efforts put forth by everybody. It was personally a major relief for me since I was given the responsibility of ensuring his recovery and with the Almighty's blessing, he recovered to his normal self.

> **Be with people when they are in distress; this means a lot to them**

There were many incidents wherein Plant Head and I were not seeing eye to eye, but we developed a habit of working together. All this came to a halt when I had to go on leave on a particular day to spend some time with my brother who had come from Australia. I was refused leave by the Plant Head without any justifiable reason. This upset me a lot considering I was a senior management staff and the second in command in the plant and knew my responsibility. I tried to reason him out but in vain. I had to bite the dust and attended duty respecting his authority, but this incident further worsened our relationship.

Skirting Tile Plant

Fortunately, by serendipity, I was then made responsible for the erection and commissioning of a tile cutting plant. This was an independent activity and kept me away from the Plant Head. The purpose of this plant was to increase the production yield by cutting skirting tiles from broken tiles. I commissioned the plant in record time and started production. Even our Plant Head was happy when we could salvage many broken tiles and convert them to saleable products.

> *Sometimes a change of assignment is beneficial to get out of a bad situation. Accept it*

CHAPTER 10

PRODUCTION DISCIPLINE THROUGH JAPANESE WORK CULTURE

"Life is what happens when you are busy making other plans"
– John Lennon

My next job was as **General Works Manager** in a new factory of a reputed paint company making industrial (automotive, white goods, marine applications) and decorative paints. A Japanese company had recently bought the majority stake in the company and was keen to bring in their work culture. Technical and Manufacturing functions were managed by Japanese Managers while the Marketing and Finance functions were managed by Indian Managers. I was reporting to the Japanese Director of Manufacturing.

The factory had 3 distinct production lines, viz. industrial, decorative, and SOD (small orders up to 100 lit). Decorative paint was more volume-oriented with not so stringent quality criteria. Industrial and SOD had very strict quality criteria in terms of shade matching. There were not many production issues in SOD as quantity is low and the worst scenario was making a new batch over again due to quality problems. But bulk production was a different story.

The Manufacturing Process

Mixing
- Titanium Dioxide, Resins & Coloured pigments are mixed in predetermined quantities

Grinding
- The above mixture is ground in a grinding mill for a predetermined time to get the Paint slurry

Thinning
- The Paint slurry is diluted with specified Solvent, Drier and Plasticizer to get various properties such as viscosity, etc.

Filtering
- The above diluted Paint slurry is filtered to remove the Paint Sludge

Packing
- The filtered Paint is packed in a container in desired quantities.

The layout of the factory is vertical with Mixing happening on the top floor, Grinding, Thinning & Filtering on the middle floors, and Packing on the ground floor. Most of the Raw material (RM) is stored on the top floor to facilitate the beginning of the production process which is Mixing. Production gets a Production Voucher (PV) from Planning for a predetermined batch size and uses the same for drawing material from stores. The PV also contains all processing details such as raw material compositions to be added in different stages of production along with the number of hours of grinding. The PV accompanies the material in various stages of processing. Production must follow the processing instructions in the PV and record the actual data in the same.

Processing of Industrial & Automotive Paints

The most critical process among the above processes for Automotive paint is grinding, wherein the colouring pigments are ground to get the required colour. We had the equipment to check matching of the colour obtained in the grinding process with the standard shade approved by the customer. Despite the above facility, the final decision regarding accepting the shade was always left to manual intervention. Even though objective matching was done by the checking equipment, there were issues with the customer and hence the manual intervention.

We had many nightmares during this stage of the process since the shade would vary based on the time of the day and there were plenty of discussions back and forth about acceptance. With the added pressure of delivering on time, this process of matching was always a challenging task. This is where process standardization for consistency in the number of hours of grinding, etc. was necessary for production.

For any new industrial shade to be supplied (automotive companies keep introducing new colours every year), once the technical department gives the PV (Production Voucher) containing the required composition of raw materials (they have lab facilities to arrive at the RM composition), a small batch is taken initially and made under the supervision of Production Engineering. The responsibility of Production Engineering is to finalize the process specification in terms of grinding hours to match the required shade as approved by the customer. This is done by trial-and-error method and the grinding hours are finalized once the actual shade is matched with the customer-approved shade. But when it comes to bulk production, the extrapolated grinding time based on the batch quantity given by Production Engineering might not give the same result for various reasons such different grinding efficiency of bigger equipment, etc.

Production Voucher Discipline

I found that Production was not following the PV given by the technical department and Production Engineering department for both raw material composition and grinding hours. They modified the RM composition and grinding hours in the PV to get the desired results. There were variations between batches in the above factors. When I enquired about this, I was told that this used to be the industry practice. I was not convinced. I further discussed this with the technical department head, and he was also agreeing with this practice. I was not comfortable with this practice as there would not be any consistency and it would be difficult to analyse in case of a quality problem because of the variation from batch to batch. It would also throw out the costing for each batch (which we were not doing but would be followed sooner) since ERP (Enterprises Resources Planning) was being implemented. I instructed that PV should be followed 100% and any problem in quality should be analysed by Production Engineering and concluded. There was a big resistance from the production team including the Production Head, but I stood my ground. As expected, there were issues at the beginning of this new practice, but Production Engineering stepped up their efforts in standardizing the PV by capturing shop floor practices. The good thing that came out of this initiative was that all recipes got corrected (which was not so earlier) and standard practices were established.

- *Always do the RIGHT thing rather than a GOOD thing for long-term benefits*
- *Process consistency is the key to consistent quality*

Decorative Paints

The challenges faced in the decorative line included increasing productivity levels measured in terms of litres per man-day as well as fulfilling the needs of customers in supplying paints in small containers. When I took over, one equipment to increase productivity levels for packing decorative paints in small containers was under trial and there were many pending issues in running it. My predecessor wanted us to give clearance towards payment for the above equipment. I took a stand that till the issues were resolved, we wouldn't give payment clearance. The supplier representative ultimately attended to most of the issues and set right the equipment. Subsequently, we could use the machine satisfactorily and got good productivity out of the equipment.

> *Never give in to pressure in any situation; Always stick to your principles and take the right decision*

Union

The new workmen in the factory were also in the nascent stages of forming a union. The management was set on having a national affiliated one that was already accepted in the parent unit. The other union was more State-driven and notorious for vandalism and work stoppages. Subsequently the union formed was the one, the management wanted.

There was a lot of misunderstanding between the management staff, right from Production Head to line supervisors, and the new workmen in terms of discipline, productivity, following safety rules, etc. The young workmen were very unhappy about the perceived unfair treatment they received at the hands of management. My job was to break this impasse and bring both together. This would make the job of transforming the team into adopting Japanese Work Culture possible as each had a role to play. Misunderstanding between the two parties would only make it more difficult.

To address this issue, I had frequent formal meetings with their unelected leaders in my office and informal meetings on the shop floor. I also ensured the team of key management personnel were with me during these meetings and allowed each of them to vent their feelings. It is always the unspoken words and hence a perceived notion that is the root cause of interpersonal relations issues. The above meetings brought a lot of issues to the table both from the management and workmen's sides and I took an impartial stand and resolved most of their issues. These ranged from proper maintenance of restrooms, provision of drinking water near the workplace, sanctioning of leaves, absenteeism without prior permission, equipment issues affecting safety & productivity, following safety rules by both staff and workmen, etc. Gradually the misunderstanding got reduced. I encouraged making small teams of line supervisors along with workmen to resolve their issues amongst themselves and approach the seniors only for want of resources.

- *Open transparent discussions always remove wrong perceptions and result in harmony both in professional and personal life*
- *Empowering teams would release their valuable time for focusing on important issues*

Through the above exercise, I developed credibility with the total team of staff and workmen. They started listening to me. I also encouraged an open-door policy and anybody with any issue can approach me without any prior appointment. My office cabin door was always kept open. Any important discussion was held in a meeting/training room.

> *Be accessible to your team to listen to their problems*

I also ensured indiscipline (like not wearing a safety helmet) was acted upon timely and fairly for both staff and workmen. I was harsh on people not wearing safety helmets, and I made them apologize to the total crowd including workmen in the section even if the culprit was a front-line supervisor.

> *Never compromise on Safety violations*

5S & Japanese Work Culture

Since we were a Just-in-Time supplier for Toyota & Ford, the emphasis on Quality was phenomenal. As per Japanese philosophy, a disciplined work culture like 5S would ensure consistent quality by following standard work procedures. Unfortunately for us, the staff and the workmen were already moulded in our way of thinking, "production over everything". Hence it was a challenge for me to change their thinking towards this new Japanese Work Culture.

We started the transformation into Japanese work culture by implementing 5S gradually.

5S

Sort	• Conduct Red Tag campaigns to identify unwanted items periodically and have a schedule to remove and dispose them
Set in orcer	• A place for everything and everything in its place - Follow a layout for materials- Keep recalibrating the layout for changing needs
Shine	• Ensure cleanliness of the work centre including the equipment. It should be possible to visually notice any abnormality in the equipment to get the same corrected.
Standardise	• Ensure consistency and continuous practice by standardising all procedures of the system
Sustain	• Ensure continuous training to all employees to follow the above steps

While the above looks simple on paper, it takes immense effort to even execute the first 2 steps since both the steps need a lot of effort from all stakeholders. The 3rd step needs commitment from the process owner to put that extra effort continuously. The 4th and 5th steps require commitment from senior management for providing resources to enable the same.

We were still in steps 2 & 3 even after lots of effort. This was how difficult it was.

> - *5S work culture results in not only good housekeeping but in good quality along with productivity and safety*
> - *Ensure all stakeholders are properly trained before implementing an initiative*

Root Cause Analysis for Non-Conformance

Our Japanese Director was very happy about the continuous efforts toward transformation. He was keen that we should address Non-Conformities (NC) and quality issues more seriously by ensuring proper Root Cause Analysis (RCA). I organized a training program in RCA for my operating staff to address his demand.

> *There are many tools of Root Cause Analysis such as Why-Why Analysis (followed by Toyota) & 8D (followed by Ford) to resolve critical management issues involving quality, maintenance, etc.*

Our Japanese Director used to comment that Indians don't admit mistakes for fear of disciplinary action and hence the same type of mistakes keeps on repeating. In Japan, all are encouraged to admit mistakes that get shared among others who would be more careful in not repeating such mistakes.

Taking a cue from the above, I stopped taking disciplinary action for mistakes of ignorance and encouraged people to admit and learn from their mistakes. I used to quote this to my team members in my subsequent assignments also. I was sending a message to everyone to admit mistakes openly and let everyone learn from these mistakes.

> *It takes real courage to admit mistakes in front of everyone, but it is worth it*

Cost Savings through Reuse

During the initial days of running the Plant, there was a lot of rejection in various processes, and the technical department was trying to salvage the rejections by accommodating them in the PV for new products. There used to be a lot of hesitation by production to follow this practice because of both the extra effort as well as the perceived risk associated in terms of creating further rejections. I started following up on these recipes and ensured most of the old rejects were salvaged and, in the process, we saved more than Rs. 1 crore. The top management was very happy about this breakthrough and started citing us as an example to other units.

> *The leader must take active participation in difficult assignments and follow through until successful completion*

Lesson from Toyota

Once our customer Toyota visited us for a periodical audit. We presented a good show. During the closing meeting, a Toyota representative mentioned that it was Toyota's practice to expect price reductions year after year from their supplier. He also mentioned that Toyota does not expect their suppliers to give price reductions by cutting their profit margin but through cost reduction efforts. This was a valuable lesson for me for my later years whenever I sat across for price negotiation.

> *Price reduction does not necessarily mean profit reduction; rather it should come out of cost reduction*

How does doing the right thing cost a Job?

As mentioned earlier, we started following recipes 100% as mentioned in PV. The technical department had substituted a raw material in one of the components of paint for cost reduction after due trials. We went ahead and started using the substitution as per the recipe in the PV. After some considerable time (Because of Just-In-Time supply, we had a practice of producing early and storing it in an intermediate warehouse and supply from there), we started receiving complaints from Toyota and Ford about serious paint defects and line stoppages. We did not realize what had happened to create this quality problem. Subsequently, on comparing good lots with problematic lots, we found that the main difference was the substituted raw material. We immediately made the paint with the original raw material and supplied the same to the customer. Due to this issue, I had to even forego visiting my mother who had a heart attack in my native place.

As already mentioned in conveyor line manufacturing, line stoppage is a crime. We were asked to submit our analysis, and corrective and preventive actions. As a Unit Head, I was also asked to go and apologize to the Toyota and Ford paint team which I did. But Toyota was not happy about this mishap and demanded stern action. In Japan, where the technical department comes under the purview of the Unit head, for any such situation, it is the Unit Head who must bear the consequences. Along the same lines, I was asked to resign. Because of my good work in the past, I was allowed to be on the payroll for a reasonable time till I got a new job. I was jobless for a short period but subsequently, I got a job. The new company took their referral from our MD who knew about my work and gave me a good reference.

> *Leadership is all about doing the right thing with a long-term view rather than compromising for short-term benefits*

Chapter 11

HANDLING A WORK STOPPAGE

"Hard things are put in our way not to stop us but to call out our
courage and strength"
– Anonymous

I joined as **Deputy General Manager** in a plastic processing company making injection moulded plastic products. The products are:

- Furniture made of low-density polyethylene (LDPE),
- Crates made of high-density polyethylene (HDPE) and
- Industrial parts for white goods such as washing machines, air conditioners, etc made of Acrylonitrile Butadiene Styrene (ABS), nylon, etc.

All the plastic parts were moulded in injection moulding machines. It had 20 such machines of various capacities. The factory also had a paint shop painting furniture and assembling them with cushions for high-end customers.

The machines were run by permanent workmen while contract workmen were engaged in the following activities namely:

a) Mixing of raw material for each moulding machine based on the product, and loading the same in injection moulding machines,

b) Removal of extra material like runners, overflown material in the edges, etc. that is part of the process in injection moulding,

c) Grinding of the extra material along with rejections,

d) Assembling various moulded and bought out components and making them ready in trolleys for Just-In-Time dispatch for Industrial Products,

e) Fabrication of crates by cutting and welding to make customized crates with partitions for industrial use,

f) Unloading of RM and loading of FG,

g) Painting of furniture & Assembly of the same with cushion materials.

The factory also had a tool room to prepare moulds in line with the production plan. The moulds were quite heavy and needed overhead cranes for handling as well as loading & unloading in the machines.

Production Challenge

The main challenge I faced in this assignment was to increase the production level which was hovering around 25 Tons per day compared to the capacity of a minimum of 40 Tons per day based on the product mix. The reasons for low tonnage were high mould changing time and frequent breakdowns of the machines.

The unreasonably high mould change time was due to reasons such as non-availability of overhead crane, mould not getting ready on time, communication gap between production and tool room team due to ego issues, quality issues in the mould, etc.

I addressed the issues of high mould change time by taking the following actions:

a) For the crane availability issue, the shift supervisors were asked to plan mould changes based on crane availability. Since the commercial plastic products were made for stock and sale, we authorized the shift engineer to over/under produce within a certain percentage (based on the lot size) of the planned quantity till the crane is available.

> *Right Empowerment motivates people and produces results*

b) To improve the mould availability on time, more fitters were recruited and added to the group. Few contractors were also engaged to do the mundane work which was otherwise consuming valuable time of the high skilled fitters. Few buffer moulds were also planned for availability as spares to fill in the waiting time for any mould-related issue if we needed to unload the mould. Root cause analysis for the mould issues was done, and corrective and preventive actions were taken.

> - *Do not waste skill in mundane activities*
> - *Keep more people than required in high-skill areas even at the cost of increased headcount*

c) The communication issue was addressed through daily stand-in meetings on the shop floor while analysing machine-wise production delays. I used to shout at the team for their inefficiencies but provided solutions and resources for resolving the issues causing the delays. I addressed their ego issues openly and ensured their open communication and commitments in daily meetings. This brought transparency and accountability. It also brought out a lot of underlying issues including interpersonal relationships, and we resolved them to not affect the production.

> *The best way to deal with interpersonal issues is through open discussions to vent out stakeholders' perceptions. Transparency always brings people closer and brings out any inner agenda*

Gradually the mould change time had improved to reach the target time and the production tonnage started improving.

The frequent breakdowns in machines were happening due to

- Improper upkeep of hydraulic power packs resulting in leaks leading to pressure drop,
- Improper cooling in control panels resulting in PCB (Printed Circuit Boards) getting heated up and malfunctioning, etc.
- Lack of skill required to address electronic problems such as malfunctioning of PCB as only one engineer could address these issues,
- Non-availability of spares for both hydraulic power packs as well as PCBs.

I had a detailed discussion with the central engineering head who sat at the corporate office and ensured spare availability regarding hydraulic power packs to bring down the downtime of the equipment.

Since few of the machines that were imported and very old had issues of getting spares such as PCB, I encouraged the electronic engineer to develop a local source for making these PCB spares. I assigned one more engineer to get trained with him in electronic maintenance. I also ensured the preventive maintenance (PM) schedule was adhered to strictly without any deviation to ensure the upkeep.

The above actions increased the daily tonnage from mid-twenties to mid-thirties, and we were achieving close to 90% of the capacity.

Industrial Customers

This company was a JIT (Just-In-Time) supplier for a customer making washing machines, and we needed to supply trolleys filled with plastic parts every 4 hours. Any delay in supply would lead to line stoppage.

During my meeting with this customer for the first time after I had joined, they mentioned as a grievance that less focus was given on supply of their parts due to lower tonnage of these parts. I committed to them that they would not have any room for complaint in future regarding timely quality supply. I ensured the above through proper focus and resources getting allocated towards the same for timely delivery.

> *Every customer is important and deserves equal treatment*

Grievance of Contractors

Our payments to contractors were based on dispatch figures rather than based on the work they had done during a period. This was due to the company's principle of sharing the revenue with stakeholders when there is a sale. But this also led to contractors getting low payments during times of low sales thereby struggling to pay wages to their workmen. They used to get loans from the local market at atrocious interest rates, and in the process, barely made their ends meet. This was one of their main grievances.

To resolve the above, I intervened with accounts and arranged for them to get advance payments against their bills during the lean period of sales. This had brought them immense relief financially, and they remained committed to me and hence the successes that followed in the organization.

> *Do not neglect any stakeholder irrespective of their status since any chain is only as strong as its weakest link*

Cost Reduction

We were also fabricating partitioned HDPE (High Density Polyethylene) crates to be used for the storage of industrial components. We used to send these crates outside for fabrication and used to lose money because of the transportation cost both ways. We also did not have control over the delivery schedule as we were not sure what was happening in the subcontractor's shop.

I organized a dedicated area inside our factory to get the fabrication done. The rates with the contractor were reduced for using in-house facility and we now also avoided transportation costs leading to huge savings overall. Added to the above cost-benefit, we started having control over production and hence delivery.

> *Internal subcontracting is always beneficial*

Premium Furniture Production

As earlier indicated, we also had a paint shop to paint the plastic furniture and assemble them with cushions to cater to the premium market segment. Since this shop was catering to the premium segment, a lot of focus was given by top management towards the output as well as the cost. We had a conveyor system to get the furniture painted continuously. This system very much resembled a conveyor line manufacturing, and any problem in quality, maintenance, etc. would stop the line. Here, I ensured PM along with timely replacement of conveyor elements to ensure continuous operation resulting in better output levels. There were lots of initiatives taken in this section on a continuous basis to bring down the cost such as alternate vendor sourcing for cushions and fabric.

> *Cost reduction is a continuous activity*

Scrap Recovery and Reuse

In almost every meeting with the owners and my boss, there was one review regarding the reuse of the scrap generated in the process. The scrap used to be from

a) extra material removed during finishing operation,

b) runners and risers which were part of the moulding process but removed after the moulding was done and

c) rejected products due to quality issues.

The reason behind this persistent review was that there was big money tied up in this scrap due to the high cost of material which is approximately 70% of the overall cost breakup of the product. Judicious usage of recovered scrap could increase the profit. Our technical specification of raw material composition allowed us to add a percentage from the recovered scrap without compromising quality. We were missing this opportunity if we were not reusing the scrap.

Our scrap yard where all varieties of scrap material were stored was located next to the recovery section. The contractor who was managing the scrap yard was very irregular and due to his negligence as well as ours, there was a lot of scrap accumulation, some of them in mixed-up condition. I called the contractor and asked him to provide manpower consistently. I gave him deadlines for completing the task of segregation of the mixed-up material and grinding them to enable it to be used in production. I had also warned him that we would engage an alternate contractor if he continued to neglect the job. He had some payment issues, and I talked with our accountant to clear his backlog payments. This incentivized him to do the job more seriously. I made him report to me directly on the progress of segregation and grinding daily to bring more seriousness to the job. Soon we had brought the scrap yard under control by clearing all accumulated scrap. I was told by the accountant that we had started making profit month after month because of the scrap usage and that is how scrap reuse was critical for making profit.

> *There is good money in reprocessing and reusing, though often overlooked*

Union

While production and scrap issues were being attended to, I also addressed a lot of pending issues related to workmen and gained their trust and established credibility with them. A section of workmen (unelected leaders) wanted to start a union. I encouraged them to have a Works Committee, but they were not very comfortable and wanted to bring an external party. I tried to convince them that it is in their best interest to have a union among themselves. This also would be acceptable to the management when it comes to wage negotiation. They said that they could trust me to take care of their interests, but they were not sure what would happen when I was not there. There were a lot of discussions back and forth, but I never gave in to their request to accept an external leader. We had the help of an IR (Industrial Relations) consultant who was a retired labour commissioner whom we were regularly consulting with on all IR-related issues. He was also advising strongly against accepting an external leader.

In the meanwhile, wage revision became due. The leaders refused to come for discussions saying that they would discuss only in the presence of their external leader. I refused flatly saying that external people had no stake in the process. They were trying to convince the workmen for drastic action like work stoppage. Anticipating the problem, I ensured that we had made enough stocks for a week's requirement of the JIT supplies by redeploying resources from other product lines.

> *We need to keep our ears to the ground in situations where industrial relations are strained and should anticipate adverse reaction and be prepared to face them*

Work Stoppage

One fine day the workmen did a sit-in strike in the workplace. I kept my cool and did not invite them for discussion. As time passed, the leaders became restless and started approaching me. I told them to start the work saying that discussions could not happen at the threat of work stoppage, and they refused. I also didn't relent in discussions.

The next day, through our General Manager who had good relations with the local police and administration, we arranged for the police to get the workmen picked up for obstructing work when they stopped the supplies towards JIT supply, and they were all let free outside the factory. In the meanwhile, we had got an injunction order from the court for not permitting the workmen within 500 meters of our plant to protect the properties of the plant. We had also suspended the union leaders pending inquiry for unjustified stopping of work.

I had already arranged with all the contractors to provide sufficient people in case of such a scenario. I asked my operating staff and office staff to come to the factory the next day prepared to stay inside the factory for at least a week. I also made cooking arrangements for all the staff and contract workmen inside the factory to prevent us from going out to avoid facing any unpleasant incident with the workmen.

We started the equipment one by one with the help of shift engineers and contract workmen, and out of 20 machines, we could start 5 machines on the first day. Our MD expressed his appreciation for starting the machines. Gradually, in the days to come, we managed to start all the machines. Production suffered initially due to operating as well as quality issues because of contract workmen running the machines. Ultimately, we managed to bring normalcy to a good extent with the help of operating staff.

> *Treat contract people as stakeholders, give them due respect and recognition, and they become a strong tool in your hands to address any adverse extreme situation*

Customer Concern

I got a call from our customer who was getting our JIT supplies during the above work stoppage. They were concerned about their uninterrupted supplies, but I explained to them my elaborate plan to deal with the same. I assured them that their supply would not get affected. There was not a single instance of delay, and their line was never stopped for want of supplies.

Pressure tactics

In the meanwhile, we got lot of pressure from the union to settle the matter. One such incident was when one of the union members (who happened to be very close to me) lodged a police complaint against me. He complained that I have scolded him using his caste name which happened to be an offense under the non-bailable act. We got a call from the police inspector in charge of such complaints (I understand that this is a special posting under the Central Government). We took all the documents to prove the malintent behind this complaint and requested him to close the complaint. He said that he could not close the complaint but promised that he would not initiate any action.

The union spoke to the contractors to withdraw their support to dilute our stand, but the contractors stood behind us for all the support we had given them in the past regarding their payment and other issues. I was warned by some well-wishers that some of them were planning to attack me and another senior colleague, but better sense prevailed in the end.

The work stoppage continued for **47 days,** and we didn't relent. Ultimately, they all agreed to our condition of not having to associate with an external party and were ready to settle the wages with us. They also wanted no penal action against the workmen for the work stoppage. We took consent forms from each of them so that they would not indulge in such activities in future. We agreed to take back all workmen but for the union leaders, whom we were ready to pay a one-time settlement for them to resign. New leaders came forward and we had a wage settlement. We also settled a one-time settlement for the old union leaders but for the one who went to court.

The above scenario of handling the work stoppage successfully would not have been possible without the support of the staff, contractors and contract workmen who kept the production going. Also, we got excellent support from top management as well as our IR consultant with his vast experience in handling such work stoppages.

Focus on Human Resources Development for workmen. This would reduce the IR situation a great deal

After the above incident, I was promoted as **General Manager**.

CHAPTER 12

CAREER IN AN INDIAN MULTINATIONAL

"Life is like a box of chocolates.
You never know what you are going to get"
– Forrest Gump

I was referred by one of my ex-colleagues for a senior position in Manufacturing in one of the most prestigious Indian Multinational companies. I joined them as **Deputy General Manager - Manufacturing** in their Rubber Processing Machinery business. The products that were being manufactured were tyre processing machinery such as Mechanical Tyre Curing Presses, Tyre Building Machines, Bias Cutting Machines, etc.

The Manufacturing Process

Profile Cutting
- The necessary profiles are cut from steel plates in CNC profile cutting machines using a software for determining the optimum combination of profiles to get the maximum yield

Fabrication
- The above cut profiles are welded along with the castings, in-house and in vendor's place resulting in the fabricated structures of various parts of a tyre processing machinery

Machining
- The fabricated structures, castings and forgings are machined in our machine shop as well and in our vendors' premises

Assembly
- The machined components along with other bought out items involving mechanical, piping, electrical and electronic parts were assembled in our assembly section

Testing
- The completed assembly is offered for testing of various functional tests

Packing
- The tested presses are dismantled as subassemblies or parts based on their size and packed in wooden crates. Smaller presses are dispatched as a whole

Machine Shop Head

I was made in charge of a machine shop that included giant Computer Numerically Controlled (CNC) machines, and I reported to the Manufacturing Head. Three section heads were reporting to me, and they were handling the Lathe section, the CNC boring machines section & Production Engineering Section (Tools, Jigs & Fixture design along with CNC programming) respectively. While the Lathe section head was good in handling the workmen, the other two handling the

CNC Boring machine and Production Engineering were brilliant in technical matters. I started using their strengths and made the daily review meetings more effective in terms of planning and execution. I was also getting into micro details of the machine shop operation which gave me an edge in giving commitments to assembly and honouring them. I treated assembly as my internal customer by addressing their concerns such as proper finishing including deburring and gained their trust in the process.

I spent most of my time speaking with the workmen, listening to their grievances, and attending to their minimal needs. My down-to-earth approach in dealing with workmen gained me credibility among them.

> *Listening to people is key to developing and maintaining good Industrial Relations*

Night Shift Operation

During the night shift, most of the operators were working only part of the shift and slept during the balance of the shift. Even though the management was aware of this, they ignored this for better industrial relations. This factory had a history of no work stoppage for 30 plus years and this was achieved through such compromises.

> *Evaluate the long-term implications of any decision which may give short-term gains. Always stand by principles and do not dilute them in the name of pragmatism*

I started attending work on the night shift, and the workmen were embarrassed to see me on the night shift seeing them sleeping. Because of the good relationship they had with me, they asked me to stop coming in night shift. I had replied that my interest was to keep the machines running. If they would agree to my proposal of allowing the trained helpers to run the machines during the shift (the helpers were also sleeping during the night shift and I wanted to put a stop to this practice), I would stop coming in the night shift. They were initially resistant citing that the helpers running the machines would create quality as well as equipment maintenance issues but subsequently relented because of the good relationship we shared, and our Original Equipment Effectiveness (OEE) started going up.

> *Always look for opportunities for improvement and use them to achieve the desired results*

Over Time (OT) – A Win-Win Approach

Our factory worked even on Sundays for one shift to cater to the demand of the union for increased earnings through OT. The workmen must attend duty on all working days in the subsequent week to claim this OT. This way the management had ensured good attendance as against offering the workmen OT. This also helped to meet the increasing needs of production.

New Responsibility

In the meanwhile, our business received a very big order of around 150 tyre curing presses from a prestigious customer, and the top management decided to try on a customer-centric approach for this order. I was given the additional responsibility of ensuring timely availability of all components for assembly of this order, and this included expediting Profile cutting, Fabrication, castings & forgings from vendors for machining and machined components from vendors. I started interacting with all the above stakeholders to ensure the availability of components for timely assembly. I came across plenty of issues from vendors regarding their insufficient capacity, working capital, etc. With the help of my boss, who also happened to be Supply Chain Management head, and other team members, we could resolve them in time to ensure the availability of components.

> *Treat vendors as your supply partners and help them to address their concerns with whatever resources are at your disposal*

Additional Responsibility

Once the above order was completed, I was given additional responsibility for the Maintenance function. Our maintenance team was one of the best teams I had worked with in terms of calibre and capability, and all they needed was more attention and support in terms of resources. They maintained proper history cards for all critical equipment, and this data was quite helpful in identifying the cause of issues as well as taking timely corrective and preventive action. The 2 main areas of concern in the factory were CNC boring machines and overhead cranes which were both very essential in our type of heavy engineering industry.

Preventive Maintenance (PM)

The common factor influencing the performance of these 2 critical equipment was strict adherence to Preventive Maintenance. As earlier mentioned, due to OT working on Sundays, it was difficult to hand over the machines for PM. The machines were not getting handed over on other days too due to pressures of delivery of components on time.

I ensured that machine/equipment was made available as per schedule by planning for any day in the week rather than a particular day of the week which used to be the earlier practice. If the equipment were not released throughout the week, equipment was released on the last day of the week. This was possible since the machine sometimes was kept idle for want of material due to delay in receipt of fabricated structures, or castings, or breakdown in EOT (Electric Overhead Transmission) cranes, etc. This proposition helped towards the better upkeep of the equipment by timely PM. We also started an in-depth Root Cause Analysis for any major and repetitive breakdown, and this helped us to bring the downtime to a great extent. Due credit should be given to the maintenance team for their excellent maintenance of a particular CNC machine for more than 15 years without any major issues.

> *Engage the maintenance team continuously by giving them assignments on improvement as they tend to become complacent during lean times of work*

One other critical factor in maintaining CNC machines is the spare availability of PCB boards in their main console. With the help of the team, we started maintaining a stock of essential PCBs and started repairing the old ones with the help of a local vendor and kept them ready.

> *Proper spare management and equipment history card management are key tools for effective maintenance management*

The main difference in attending to mechanical and electrical/electronic breakdown is that in the former, identification of the problem is easy but attending to the problem takes time. In the latter, it takes more time to identify the problem but takes very little time to resolve.

Rating & Reward

During my tenure, I found the following discrepancies in the Performance Management Appraisal System and fought with the management to address them.

- Some employees were being given the same rating year after year irrespective of their performance just because of their high rating in the previous year,
- Employees who had cleared the leadership potential test were given higher ratings irrespective of their annual performance,
- Employees who got an opportunity to go abroad on company work were given lesser ratings since they had already earned money through their foreign trip (because of FOREX differential between Indian currency and US currency),
- Graduate Engineers and Diploma Engineers were grouped together irrespective of their grades while giving ratings despite the difference in their qualifications and calibre. Diploma engineers were being given low ratings due to this grouping and, hence getting a raw deal.

I ensured that the staff in my department were treated fairly by ranking the individuals based on their grades and that the current year's performance only. I also ensured the bell curve system was followed during my submission to Macro View Group (who had a final say in ratings) with the intent that the same ratings would be finalized. While this had brought justice to the system, employees were continuing to complain about the bell curve system of performance ratings.

- *Treat every employee as your internal customer and be fair to them*

- *Be candid in explaining to the subordinate employees about their area of improvement, and do not shirk this responsibility because of the unpleasantness of the exercise*

- *Keep a record of employees' performance throughout the year (Remember PPC in my earlier assignment) which would help assess the employee during the annual performance review*

CHAPTER 13

CHALLENGES IN FACTORY MANAGEMENT

"My job is not to be easy on people.
My job is to make them better"
– Steve Jobs

The Rubber Processing Machinery business was expanding its facilities in India as well as in China. I was asked whether I would be willing to go to China. I politely declined despite the opportunity it presented as I needed to take care of my old parents. Hence, I was asked to go to a nearby town wherein a new factory was being set up. I was asked to head this factory and I readily accepted.

This new factory is a replica of the old one but for its scope of operation. It included a machine shop consisting mostly of CNC machines, a fabrication shop, and an assembly shop with storage provision for MS (Mild Steel) plates, castings and forgings. The Stores operations were handled by a third-party agency, unlike the old shop.

The profiles for fabrication were being cut either at the old factory or at the vendor's place by supplying the MS plates from the new factory.

This new factory was planned with the idea of manning both the fabrication and assembly sections through contract employees for the apprehension of union formation later. While this was getting implemented, the same was being objected by the old factory union.

They once visited the factory and staged a "dharna" (protest) in front of the main gate regarding this. I somehow diffused the situation using the good relationship I shared with them. We still went ahead and continued to engage contract workmen.

> ***Good relationships always come in handy during times of crisis***

Our scope was to manufacture smaller presses while bigger structures were getting fabricated, machined, and sent for assembly in the old unit.

Machine Shop Operations

The manufacturing head planned that the costly CNC machines in the new factory should be operated by Diploma Engineers rather than the normal ITI (Industrial Training Institute) trained operators. This was due to the value addition they would bring later in terms of improvements in productivity, quality, and cost. There were lots of deliberations/objections among senior management as to how to differentiate these Diploma Engineers who would operate the machines from the already existing Diploma Engineers who were performing various staff activities. We had put up an argument that we would get trained Diploma Engineers who would know the intricacies of machine operations if they operated the machine. Hence, they would be better qualified to take over staffing roles including supervising the production in shops as well as performing quality assurance activities as and when a vacancy arises. We also recommended compensating them differently by giving some special allowances for operating the machine. Finally, we got the idea approved and recruited diploma engineers for this purpose.

> *Implementing new ideas always has obstacles, but do not give up*

I became the mentor of these raw diploma engineer trainees who joined us to run the CNC machines. I organized on-the-job training for these trainee engineers in the CNC machines by deputing them to our vendor premises with the help of my boss who also was heading SCM. We could not do the same in our shops in the old factory for fear of unionized workmen not accepting them and hence not imparting the training properly. We had also instructed the trainee engineers to also get trained in the maintenance issues of CNC machines to enable them to resolve the minor maintenance issues by themselves. They had been told upfront that they would be the owners of the new CNC machines for their performance. This was to bring the concept of TPM (Total Productive Maintenance) into their minds even before they started operating these machines.

> *Inculcate good habits among trainees right from day one*

The trainee engineers got trained in the vendor premises for 6 months and were brought back when the machines were getting installed and commissioned to know the basic mechanics of the machine. They were also trained in CNC programming by one of the engineers brought from the old unit. They successfully started operating the machines, and in course of time, started completing jobs in process times that were considerably lower than what was being done in the old unit. They had become our key assets.

> *Always ensure to operate your costly equipment with qualified personnel to get the best results*

Handling Politicians

As the factory head, one of my responsibilities was to handle local administrative heads. Since the plant was in a Panchayat (run by village council), I had to maintain a good relationship with the local Panchayat Head. This gentleman was pestering me to give him some contract work to enable him to get a steady income even if he would lose the upcoming panchayat elections. It would be "hara-kiri" (suicide) to get associated with the politicians in factory matters. We would not have control over the activity he was responsible for, and we would not be able to offend him by refusing him payment if he were to offer poor quality. I dodged him saying that he would need to register himself for meeting statutory obligations with various agencies like Provident Fund, Employees State Insurance, Factory inspectorate, etc as per company policy, and then only the management could consider his proposal. With this tactic, we implied that he would need to spend money to get these approvals, and he was not willing to incur any expense since he wanted easy money without any upfront investment. He kept on pestering me and I kept on dodging him quoting statutory requirements. Till my last day of the assignment, I managed to ward him off.

> *Deal with politicians diplomatically*

Planning a new layout – Key Decisions

The business was not picking up due to market conditions. A decision was taken to close the old unit because the management planned to develop the land for commercial establishments. It was decided to bring all the operations of both the old and new units under one roof. Hence, I was told to plan for shifting of all the operations from the old unit to our unit. Since we did not initially plan space for accommodating such a huge requirement, we needed to take the following key decisions.

Outsourcing Fabrication

We decided to outsource total fabrication so that the same space can be used for shifting the machine shop from the old unit. One of our colleagues who recently returned from China had taken over Supply Chain Management. With his help, we approached a prominent steel manufacturer who had expanded their operations through downward integration by setting up a shop for fabrication. This unit was around 40 kms from our unit. Since the volumes were quite high (around 700 MT per month), we got into a contract with him for fabricating our major structures with their steel plates as per our specifications. As regards the pricing of these structures, we settled the same as 2 components viz. steel price and conversion cost. While steel price was linked to the SAIL (Steel Authority of India) rate, the conversion rate was decided based on the prevailing market rate. Since the unit was close enough, we managed to have vigilance over the production and quality of our fabricated structures.

This way, we ensured that the fabrication bay was released and available for shifting the machines from our old unit. Through the above arrangement, we also managed to avoid the storage of Mild Steel plates thereby having the extra space required for the storage of components for assembly.

Harness Outsourcing as a Strategy to meet business requirements

Shifting Defence Section

We also had a defense section as part of the business that was operating independently. This was recently taken over by the defense division of the group that was in a different location. Hence, their operation which was being carried out in a separate bay in our unit was asked to be shifted to the location where the defense division was operating. Once vacated, this bay was used for assembly.

Seating Arrangement for Staff

We also modified the design of the administration block which was already under construction to accommodate the extra staff who would be shifted from the old unit.

Planning for shifting

The challenge in shifting was mainly in ensuring that none of the delivery schedules to our customers were affected during the above exercise. We had to plan in micro details, and we started the planning activity in consultation with central planning.

> *Get into micro detailing for the execution of any project since it is the little things that get ignored and derail the project deadline*

The above shifting would also lead to unplanned layout issues in terms of more WIP movement of material between the various shops such as machine shop, assembly, and paint shop. This issue could not be addressed effectively since the original layout did not plan to accommodate such an arrangement.

MLP & Promotion

In the meanwhile, I was selected to attend the Management Leadership Potential Test (MLP). Only top performers are selected for MLP, and a very small percentage of people (less than 10%) clear this very difficult test. Clearing this test would assure faster career growth inside the organization.

I approached various people who attended this test and collected valuable input about the same. The test involved evaluating competencies such as customer orientation, strategic initiatives, number crunching, people management, and business communication, etc, through various exercises such as Roleplay, Management discussion, In-tray, Business Presentation, etc. I took time from my regular work and spent considerable time familiarising myself with the above exercises to face this test. All my preparation paid off and I cleared the same.

> *Spend enough time to ensure your career growth rather than only focusing on regular work, leaving everything to chance. This includes getting that extra qualification, attending training programs to improve your competency, etc.*

Subsequently, I was promoted as **Senior Deputy General Manager**.

Change

Our company was getting into the power plant equipment business which was a sunrise industry then, and major investments were planned for setting up manufacturing facilities. The management was looking out for people to manage this new venture in various capacities. Our MD was interviewing various potential candidates personally. I was asked to appear for an interview by him. During the interview, he was impressed by my knowledge of Hindi (which I picked up in my earlier assignments) along with my history of mobility and my willingness to relocate. I was selected to join the team.

Hence, I had to leave the relocation assignment midway.

CHAPTER 14

CREATING A WORLD CLASS MANUFACTURING FACILITY

"Ulluvadhu ellam uyarvullal mattradhu
thallinum Thallamai theerthu"
– Thirukkural

(Meaning: "Keep your thoughts high and try to achieve them.
Even if they cannot be achieved, do not lose hope")

Our company was setting up new manufacturing units for making power plant equipment such as Supercritical Boilers, Pulverisers, Turbines, Air Preheaters, Axial Fans & Electrostatic Precipitators. The location that was chosen to set up these units already had an existing facility for making heavy equipment for defense, onshore and offshore projects as well as shipbuilding. The company entered a Joint Venture with a reputed Japanese firm for making Supercritical Boilers including Coal Pulverisers and Turbines. I was responsible for the Coal Pulveriser Manufacturing facility right from civil construction and I had to ensure the same was ready for production and deliver the equipment as per contract.

I was reporting to the General Manager – Pulveriser Division. The budget for making the above unit was Rs. 100 Cr.

World Class Manufacturing (WCM)

What is WCM? My understanding is that it is achieving the best manufacturing metrics in PQCDSM (Productivity, Quality, Cost, Delivery, Safety & Morale) through best practices by a competent team of people. The best practices include work culture such as 5S, Total Productive Maintenance (TPM), Total Quality Management (TQM), Digitalisation, etc. A competent team of people is achieved through practices such as Job Rotation, Multiskilling, Competency Mapping, Skill Matrix, etc.

The Team

When I joined this assignment, we already had a manufacturing team of 9 staff consisting of 2 managers with previous experience from a reputed firm, 2 engineers with a couple of years experience, along with 5 Graduate Engineer Trainees (GET) who had been recruited directly off campus. The office was temporarily established in a prefabricated container. Further recruitment was in process for the rest of the staff as well as the workmen. We were assigned a Human Resources (HR) staff from the Boiler HR (Human Resources) team to enable the recruitment process. We were to take technical help from the staff of the existing defense unit for machinery selection and infrastructure-related issues.

Work Allocation & Execution

The 2 managers were selected to head production and manufacturing engineering respectively. The managers were also responsible for the selection of machine tools & recruitment of staff and workmen, and were assisted by the 2 engineers. They were brilliant and excellent in execution skills, and along with the 5 GETs and a new QA engineer who joined shortly, we made an excellent start as a team.

I started having daily standing meetings with the small team in the morning outlining the plan for the day. Each GET was given exclusive responsibility namely

- Civil construction activities,
- Planning and ensuring arrival of the Prefabricated structures for the shop to facilitate erection as and when civil works were completed,
- Facility Planning & Procurement towards plant infrastructure,
- Assisting with the Selection of Machine Tools and
- Selection of Tooling.

All the GETS were working under the guidance of the two managers. I was driving all of them with target dates for each activity bringing in result orientation. I became famous for asking completion dates for every activity. We had prepared a Gantt chart and displayed the same for various activities with target dates for completing each activity for regular monitoring of the project.

Other staff like Planning Head, Machine shop head, Assembly head, QA head, Maintenance head, Manufacturing engineers and shift engineers along with store person were recruited gradually, and everybody was ingrained with the idea of having a World Class Manufacturing facility right from day one.

Layout to maximize production space

The two managers and I were jointly planning the layout of the factory incorporating various facilities. During this exercise, we ensured the positioning of all production accessories such as coolers and distribution switchboards in between the columns so that no production space under the crane area was wasted. We also used vertical space through mezzanine floors in between the columns to house the power panels for the proposed machines while locating the tools and consumables storage underneath the same.

> *Ensure the most optimum and efficient usage of factory space including vertical space utilization*

We provided enough space in our factory to accommodate a training room under the crane parking area without wasting any valuable production space. We also planned a meeting room and shop floor offices in between the columns to seat all shop floor personnel such as planning and production section heads (They were otherwise planned to be seated in the Administration block which is 500 metres away). All the accommodations were done within the allotted budget.

> *Ensure all operating staff are located close to their operations*

I also instructed that no glass window in the shop floor offices was to be covered by any impediment like paper or a shelf to enable an uninterrupted view of the production activities.

> *Ensure 100% visibility in factory operations*

I kept a small office for myself on the shop floor even though I had an office in the Administration block. I used this factory office to meet shop floor employees to listen to them during my daily visit to the plant in the morning and afternoon, or sometimes even during the night shift which I did as a surprise inspection.

> *Be in continuous touch with the front-line team to understand the ground reality*

Independent Work Centres

I ensured the provision of a few localized crane facilities (which were not provided in the budget) like monorail cranes for specific work centres so that there was no loss in production waiting for EOT (Electric Overhead Transmission) cranes. This was mainly due to my experience in my earlier assignment wherein machines would be waiting for EOT cranes resulting in low operational efficiency.

> ***Make every work centre as independent as possible***

We were also helped by the local team from the existing facility along with the local Administrative Head for selection of machine tools for our facility. The local Administrative Head was also very helpful with many of our activities including statutory clearances, etc. He used to take a physical inspection round of the site along with us every Thursday and addressed any issues related to construction on the spot. The ordering for all items was done by the Purchasing Team of the Boiler unit since we did not have our team in place.

Recruitment & Training

We recruited fresh ITI trainees such as **Fitters** for Assembly & Maintenance, **Machinists** for Machine Shop, and **Electricians** for Maintenance. Once the recruitment of these ITI trainees was completed, we signed a Memorandum Of Understanding with the local National Institute of Technology (NIT) for training them further in the classroom as well as in their workshop.

We kept monitoring their progress every week. During my visits to the campus, I used to address them and kept brainwashing them on how to make a World Class Manufacturing Facility and how they can contribute towards the same. I wanted them to enter our factory with the same mindset to attain our common goal of establishing a World Class Manufacturing Facility.

> *Plant your ideas with team members in the early stages of enterprise to enable easy implementation*

I deputed a couple of my graduate engineer trainees from the next batch for 6 months to my previous organization, the rubber processing machinery unit. I wanted them to get hands-on training in the maintenance of the CNC machines including CNC control panels. As already mentioned, the maintenance team of this unit was the best one I had come across. This gave a good opportunity for the young engineers to learn from the best. My relationship with the old team made it possible for them to accommodate these trainees and train them effectively. When the machines were erected and commissioned, we had trained engineers on hand to handle any maintenance issues. I had also instructed these engineers to keep in touch with their trainers to discuss any difficult maintenance issue they might come across, and this was very helpful for them to discharge their duties effectively.

> *Continuous networking is always beneficial*

Shift Meeting and Communication

When our shop was ready, we instituted a physical exercise session at the beginning of each shift for both staff and workmen (A Japanese practice). I also participated in the exercise session of the General shift.

We also used these sessions for important communications. These sessions started with the swearing of the safety slogan by every member. Any news good or bad was shared in these sessions and every team member was kept informed of anything relevant to the operation of our unit. These included new customer orders, customer complaints, planning of customers and other VIP visitors, safety incidents including near-miss, and accidents if any. This was a very powerful forum, and it took approximately 15 min of our valuable production time, but it was worth every minute.

> *Open communication helps continuous employee engagement*

Safety

The amount of importance we gave to safety was so much that every one of the members was breathing safety. We instituted a system of recording all safety incidents which could have led to accidents. We ensured that any safety incident had to be attended to on priority and I was personally monitoring for CAPA (Corrective and Preventive actions). While the boiler shop had a separate safety head with a team (one of them was assigned to our unit), I emphasized that every shop engineer is a safety engineer, and every workman is a safety representative. I never entered the shop without safety PPE. We also ensured that anybody who violated safety rules irrespective of the position held in the factory should apologize in public. During my surprise night visits, when I saw any engineer without PPE (Personal Protective Equipment), I made him publicly apologize to the team including the workmen. Some of the engineers were upset about this but that was the way I had shown my seriousness and imbibed a safety culture.

> *Set yourself as an example and show conviction in any initiative. Walk the talk*

M/s. Dupont was one of the companies in the world in adopting the best safety culture. They have a very thorough audit system for assessment of safety and many organizations were engaging them professionally the world over. Their staff visited our whole campus for an assessment of all units regarding safety. Our unit was appreciated by them for the special efforts we had deployed for imbibing a safety culture. Our success was reflected in that we were the only ones in the audit to score above 80 while all the other units scored in the ranges of 60s and 70s.

As per DuPont 's recommendation, all of us had to go through a behaviour-based safety training program. I encouraged many of my engineers to become trainers themselves to spread this culture to the total campus. This training was different from the normal safety training program as it went beyond individuals following safe work practices; it included counselling others to follow as well. This also included recording all observations related to safety which we were already following. I even set a target for all staff and workmen including myself to record a minimum of one safety observation per month per employee.

> *Any good initiative needs to start at the top*

Inauguration of Assembly

We completed the construction of the assembly shop in a record 9 months, thanks to the consistent drive by the Chairman of our company through his weekly visits. Our Procurement section had developed vendors to supply the machined forgings, castings, fabricated structures (since our machine shop was not yet ready), and other bought-out items. We inaugurated our assembly shop by making the first subassembly of the Pulveriser in the 10th month from the day of Bhoomi Puja (an inaugural fire ceremony of the Earth before commencement of any construction) with our trained set of workmen and staff.

> *A good Leader always drives his team towards achieving challenging results*

Inauguration of Machine Shop

As regards the machine shop, all the CNC machines barring drilling machines were imported. The delivery of these machines took 12 to 16 months with the added time of ½ a month to 1 ½ months for erection and commissioning. One of the prime factors for selecting machinery other than budget was delivery, and we made sure that we got the best delivery terms. I visited all the vendors who were in Europe and personally monitored the progress to ensure the vendors meet their commitments on delivery. When the machines got ready, we sent our engineers to their shops for inspection, and this was an additional benefit for those engineers, who had joined our company, for an opportunity to work abroad briefly. Of course, as per company policy, all of us had to agree to a bond of serving the company for a minimum period of 3 years to compensate for the money spent on the international trip.

We started receiving the machines one by one, and successfully erected and commissioned them on time. The machine shop was completed in 18 months which was a record for such a machine shop considering the huge size of the machines we were ordering. In coordination with our procurement group, we ensured receiving the unmachined forgings, castings, and fabricated structures for machining in our shop on time. We became a full-fledged production shop in 18 months. I consider this entire assignment a huge success and will always be proud about it.

Job Rotation

We used Diploma Engineers for supervising the shop floor while the key activities like Planning, Manufacturing Engineering, and Quality were being handled by Graduate engineers. During their training period of 1 year, they were rotated every 3 months among the various sections. After confirmation, they were assigned to a particular section.

I instituted an additional system of job rotation in which the engineers were transferred to an internal supplier section or internal customer section after every 2 years. This was done to ensure that they understood the difficulties of all the stakeholders they were dealing with. This had brought good understanding and appreciation of each function which ultimately led to good teamwork. I was monitoring this personally as there was always hesitation from the section head to let go of one of their experienced team members and accept a new one in his place.

> *Never allow a person to settle in a job since the same would lead to complacency*

Competency Mapping

We started competency mapping for all the staff with the help of the HR staff (the same staff who was recruiting for us). I made him do a lot of groundwork in this exercise, and without his help and involvement, this initiative would not have been so effective. We used this competency mapping to plan training programs for our staff for which our company was very famous in terms of the resources it deploys to Training & Development (We have a dedicated Leadership Development Academy). Such is the importance given to Training & Development.

Skill Matrix & Multiskilling

With the help of the QA Head, we designed a skill matrix for workmen, listing necessary skills for each function like assembly, machining, and maintenance. We started mapping each workman against the standards set for each of the skills. Based on the mapping and the gaps found in the skills, we then arranged training for these workmen on all the necessary skills by our staff as well as the staff from nearby units of our company. The training room we had planned for earlier inside our shop came in handy. Every workman had undergone this training compulsorily, and it was the responsibility of the respective Section Head to ensure they did so. Each of the workmen was tested every quarter through both written tests and interviews conducted by the QA team, and their skill matrix was updated accordingly. This was a continuous activity till each of the workmen achieved competent levels in each of the skills mapped.

We used this model to make internal transfers among sections to give the workmen an opportunity in multi-skilling. Our QA team played a great role in this activity, and this was well appreciated by all visiting Dignitaries along with our JV partner.

- *Quantification of skill leads to a better comprehension of the same*
- *Facilitating continuous improvement and skill building on the job not only helps in the career growth of individual employees but is also powerful for improved company performance*

The Kaizen Culture

We tracked our factory performance by measuring PQCDSM (Productivity, Quality, Cost, Delivery, Safety & Morale not necessarily in the same sequence). Kaizen means small and continuous improvements undertaken in the workplace with the involvement of all employees with a goal of significant improvements in the longer run. We started the Kaizen movement in the shop to improve the above factors by involving all the employees in it.

A standard format in both English and the local language was kept on the shop floor for easy accessibility. Staff or workmen who had ideas or suggestions regarding improving any of the above parameters could fill the forms and submit the same in drop boxes kept for the purpose. We developed a system of rewarding people in small ways such as offering pens, chocolates, key chains, and wallets to encourage participation. Soon, we started receiving numerous ideas where the Kaizen philosophy could be applied.

A Kaizen committee was formed to evaluate and prioritize these ideas for Kaizen and give recommendations for implementation. Whenever a Kaizen idea could not be implemented, we called the member who had given the idea and gave him the rationale behind the decision to avoid any disappointment. I had set a target of one implemented Kaizen per employee per month, and this went into their performance appraisal systems as well. Kaizen ideas regarding safety were implemented as priority. Subsequently, we had a Kaizen organization in place headed by the Manufacturing Engineering Head whose key role was improvement in factory operations.

> *Continuous improvement through self-contribution leads to pride & work satisfaction*

I was insistent that empty Kaizen forms should be available near every workstation. This was needed to be done to ensure that every idea was getting recorded immediately before the focus shifted back to routine job leading to the idea being missed. The emphasis was so much so that finally, we ended up keeping a box full of Kaizen forms in every alternate column in the shop to have easy accessibility and ready availability.

> *Always facilitate to ensure a successful implementation of any initiative*

We also sent our engineers, trainees, and workmen to participate in a state-level Kaizen competition wherein they brought accolades to the company by winning many prizes. Being a new company, there was no policy yet to send workmen out of town (engineers and trainees were allowed to travel), and our HR was having reservations. However, I was determined in sending the workmen and had my way by making the HR draft a policy that allowed for travel of workmen as well.

> *There is always a first time to starting a new practice*

We regularly sent our engineers including trainees to technical exhibitions across the country to get exposed to the latest technology. Once they completed a visit, each employee or the team involved had to take up an improvement project based on their observations in the exhibition and demonstrate the practical application of the knowledge they acquired. I always encouraged them to think differently even at the cost of a few mistakes which, I explained to them, was the cost of learning. I considered training & development as investments in **Human Capital** rather than an expense as per our accounting standards.

> *Practical Application of Knowledge results in the culmination of the same*

Our Japanese JV partner deputed one of their engineers to our shop on a permanent basis, and he kept reporting to his boss back in Japan about the progress in our shop (a similar arrangement was there for the boiler shop as well). He was relaying some of these Kaizens to Japan for implementation in their units. Such was the tremendous impact we had from our Kaizen movement.

Non-Conformance & Root Cause Analysis

In discussion with the QA head, we organized a training on Root Cause Analysis (RCA) for all our engineers. I insisted that RCA should be done for any major Non-compliance in Quality, Safety, and Maintenance functions. Initially, the engineers had a lot of hesitation as this involved collecting and recording data in a systematic way and looking for long-term solutions to the problems rather than short-term actions. Generally, Indians who are very intelligent but very poor at recording tend to solve the problems in their head and hence the knowledge never gets shared. The above proposed practice was different in that every detail had to be put in writing and the process was much more transparent and formalized than implementing solutions from an individual's head. It also created a valuable database for future use. This was a major culture change and hence the resistance that accompanied. I repeatedly explained to my team that in a World Class Setup, it was all about learning continuously and sharing the learnings through such records. Slowly they came around, and RCA became our way of life.

> *QC Tools are important for improvement in operations*

Works Committee

During the first year of operation, I constituted a Works Committee in the Pulveriser shop much to the discomfort of many members of the Boiler team including a few seniors. This Works Committee consisted of representatives from each section both on the staff and workmen side. They were supposed to meet every fortnight to discuss the working conditions and other operational issues. This was headed by the Production Head along with the HR staff assigned to our shop. I attended a few initial sessions to set the ball rolling.

The workmen and their supervisors were encouraged to bring out any issues that came in the way of a good working relationship between them. Initially, there were heated discussions. Subsequently, they started having fruitful discussions, and many of the petty issues which were irritants were handled. These issues ranged from provision of drinking water, cleanliness of toilets, sanctioning of leaves, simple disciplinary issues, etc. I made sure that these sessions were in practice till the last day of the assignment. The impact of this initiative was that while the whole campus, including Boiler, was not cooperating in the workplace during wage negotiations, our shop workmen had committed to us that they would not create any discomfort in the shop even though they agreed with the others in principle.

> *Facilitate partnership between supervisors and workmen for a better work environment*

5S & Housekeeping

We arranged for training in 5S (Refer to chapter 10 for details) for the entire team and maintained high standards of housekeeping in our factory. I remembered our division director mentioning that a plant's housekeeping reflects the character of the Plant Head, and I took it to heart. We ensured that we followed the principles of 5S rigorously. Each area in the factory, including toilets, was assigned to different individuals with their photos displayed in the area. Even I was allocated to an area, and I ensured proper housekeeping in that area through my daily visits. I also made it a point to use the factory toilet during my daily factory visit to ensure that it was maintained with high housekeeping standards. I used to throw tantrums for any lack of attention to safety and housekeeping so much so that the daily verbatim among staff would be "who would be the scapegoat today to get a bashing from the unit head". However, one of my strengths is that once the moment of outburst is passed, I tend to forget about it and move on. In such situations, I used to immediately crack a joke to lighten the mood and bring back the situation to normalcy. In this way, I managed to keep the morale high while condemning any shortcoming.

A Visual Factory

I wanted our factory to be a visual one and therefore ensured displays for most of the activities so that everything was self-explanatory and gave employees the information they needed, where and when they needed it.

We had a display board near the entrance to the factory giving the trend of PQCDSM. The board also displayed the progress of the Kaizen movement along with Kaizen statistics. We also displayed the status of the skills of workmen through the skill matrix expressed as a Spider Web.

Every work centre had displays about
- the specification of the machines,
- details of the job being done, and the next job planned,

- performance of the work centre in terms of Productivity, Quality, Delivery, and Safety,
- the person responsible for 5S,
- Preventive Maintenance schedule of the work centre along with OEE and MTBF (Mean Time Between Failure)
- Person responsible for maintaining the displays.

Visual Attendance Board

Our factory was also equipped with a visual attendance board near the entrance showing the organizational chart of the factory using passport size photos. If the photo was visible in the chart, it meant the person was physically present inside the factory; else it was turned backward and filled with details such as off duty, on leave, or tour with the necessary box ticked by a pencil with an eraser kept near the board. Any person who entered our shop could know who all were physically present inside the shop at any point in time. Our safety-in-charge was very happy about this as this used to be one of the main requirements for any emergency like a fire accident, etc.

> *While computers are good for data storage and analysis, visual displays are good for awareness regarding the actual (present) vs target (future)*

Total Productive Maintenance (TPM)

Once we had stabilized production, safety, 5S, Kaizen, etc., we started a TPM movement in our shop. Usually, the practice is to engage an external consultant (who charges exorbitant fees) and implement TPM, but we started with whatever expertise we had.

We had been already focusing on 5S, Quality Maintenance (through RCA), Training & Education (through competency mapping and skill matrix), SHE, and Planned Maintenance (through Preventive Maintenance). Hence, we decided to focus on Autonomous Maintenance, Focused Improvement, Early Equipment Management, and Office TPM pillars. Separate CFT (cross-functional teams) were put together for each pillar and monthly reviews were done to monitor the progress.

We bought many toolsets for workmen to enable **Autonomous Maintenance** by the operator themselves for all minor maintenance work. The operator was supposed to start the shift by checking the machine for any abnormality using a checklist. We had to ensure that the operator's time was effectively spent in the above activity to ensure good productivity of the machine. This was done by following a proper sequence of checkpoints for daily inspection of the equipment by workmen. Even the optimum route to be taken by the operator around the machine was carefully planned so as not to waste any time. I would like to express my special appreciation to one engineer who had shown extraordinary dedication in terms of implementing this pillar. He was keenly involved in the training of the workmen, planning of the inspection checkpoints for each machine, etc. to make the pillar a success.

In the **Focused Improvement** pillar, projects such as reduction of set-up time in CNC machines, Reduction in the lead time of supplying components to assembly, etc. were addressed successfully.

We also bought Predictive Maintenance kits such as vibration analysers, etc. to address the **Early Equipment Management** pillar.

As regards the **Office TPM pillar**, 5S was implemented in all our offices to ensure efficient storage of all records and files for fast and easy retrieval as well as timely disposal of obsolete and unwanted documents.

In the meanwhile, our JV partner had sent technical teams consisting of their plant personnel to both Boiler and Pulveriser shops to undertake improvements. When they visited the Pulveriser shop, they reported back that we were way ahead in improvements and did not need any help from their side. They had focused only on Boiler shops for improvements.

Pulveriser shop had become a model shop in all facets of manufacturing on the campus (that consisted of around a dozen shops) in terms of 5S, Kaizen, TPM, etc. to achieve PQCDSM.

> *Improvement is a continuous journey. Ride the same to add value to the organization*

Manufacturing Engineering

Our manufacturing engineering was one of the key functions toward the success of our unit. They had been given only one directive by me. The operator should only follow the instructions 100% given in the form of process sheets for each operation on a component. No time should be lost towards any doubt on the part of the machine operator while undertaking the operation. Fortunately, I got an excellent engineer manager who rose to the challenge and delivered. He also developed a team out of the engineer trainees to carry on the task. They had been given stiff targets for productivity improvement through tooling towards reduction in machining time and through fixtures towards reduction in set-up time respectively. They were also responsible for any quality issues that had arisen due to their process sheets. I would challenge them continuously with crazy ideas and in response, they came up with sound ideas for improvement. One of their engineers was so good that he was recruited by our tooling supplier for his deep knowledge of tools used in machining. Other than normal responsibilities, Manufacturing Engineering was also responsible for implementing Kaizens regarding productivity. They also played a key role in our Kaizen movement and were a key part of the Kaizen organization.

> *Always have a separate set-up for process improvements to have focused efforts*

Financial Crisis & Marginal Costing

Once we completed the initial orders, there was a dearth in orders due to stiff competition in the market, and we started having spare capacity. I took the initiative and approached other units in the campus for their machining requirements. I was offering them the rates they were giving to their current vendors even though our machine hour rate was far higher than the prevailing market rates due to the heavy depreciation involved in new machinery. I decided that even if we get a rate that was more than our variable expenses, I would be able to have a positive cash flow towards covering part of our fixed expenses. Our accountants (common with Boiler) were objecting to this, but I argued that I would be getting some extra cash flow rather than drain the same. I also emphasized that my team would be busy operating the machines rather than remaining idle which has its significant problems. We started receiving orders for machining from our sister units. We got a prestigious order for machining one important component for a nuclear reactor. While this order had taught us a lot in terms of the challenges faced in machining a highly accurate job, it also made us decent money. This way I could cover part of the fixed expenses in running my shop during a lean period.

> - *Engage people continuously to keep their morale high*
> - *In business, cash flow is equally important as profit*

In the meanwhile, I was promoted to **Joint General Manager** after an interview with our Division Director, and he was very appreciative of my efforts in making a World Class Manufacturing Facility.

Chapter 15

TURNING AROUND A BUSINESS

"I always think in life passion supersedes everything"
– Bret Michael's

As part of recognition of my performance and my career growth, I was transferred as **Chief Executive (CE)** to head a Joint Venture Company with a Danish partner. This company had a turnover of Rs. 60 Cr which was small by our corporate standards. It had already lost its net worth to the extent of Rs. 18 Cr from the initial share capital of Rs. 120 Cr since its inception 4 ½ years ago. Its products Axial fans and Air Preheaters are auxiliary equipment to Boilers and were important to our Power division's capability to supply all equipment for a power plant under one roof.

Our JV partner was a pioneer and world market leader in these product segments. Marketing, Project Execution, HR, and Finance functions were managed by Indian Managers while Engineering, Production Operations, Purchase & After Sales services were managed by the JV partner's representatives.

The factory was located where all our power plant manufacturing units including Boiler and Pulveriser manufacturing units were located. Finance, Engineering, Project execution, Purchase & HR functions were operating from a different location sharing the same premises as the Boiler's similar functions. Overnight, my ex-boss became my key customer. We also catered to other boiler manufacturers in India.

I joined as the 5th CE for this company for its 5th year of operation and it can be understood how changing leadership could have affected the performance of this organization. This was a sore point for the JV partner who complained continuously that Indian management was not serious enough to ensure continuity of top leadership.

Operating Location

I had to initially decide where to operate from because of the dual location set-up the company had. The current location wherein I already had a settled family life was attractive because of the location itself, and this was where the Marketing Head was also operating from. The other location was close to my key customer as well as having all other functions such as engineering, purchase, project execution, and human resources. Also, the JV partner's representatives namely the COO (Chief Operating Officer) & CTO (Chief Technology Officer) were operating from the other location.

I realized that if I had to build a close relationship with the JV partner as well as ensure timely project execution which was a key issue by then, I had to relocate to the other location and hence I decided accordingly.

> *Follow Gemba (Workplace) principle to solve problems. Physical presence in a problematic area makes a big difference in a positive way*

Work Culture

I was surprised to notice that there was no time discipline in the new location, and most of the staff were always late for work with even the COO & CTO coming late for work. I used to be the first one to enter the office even though I used to leave on time most of the days after the office hours were over. Immediately after taking over as CE, I emphasized on discipline and ensured that staff should be at their work desk on time. I communicated that any late coming would be considered as half a day leave or absent if leave is not available (This rule was existing but was not followed strictly earlier). Soon most of the staff became punctual.

> *Discipline is the starting point for any journey towards a goal*

I started holding the morning standing meeting for all staff by 9.15 am (the office starts at 9 am) to communicate the key aspects of our business including new orders, customer complaints, site issues, etc.

Teamwork

The main issue of this company was lack of teamwork and playing blame games against each other - Project execution blaming Engineering, Purchase blaming Project Execution, and Engineering for lack of information for completing PO (Purchase Order) on time, etc. In the process, the projects were getting delayed. They did not even discuss the issues across the table. Rather, they were using email for communication with each other despite working in the same office and using the same for covering their back. I put a full stop to this email communication instructing that email should be strictly used only for information sharing and any clarification should be sought in person by walking to the next table (I even discouraged using their intercom phones initially as I wanted them to meet face to face and discuss and resolve).

> *Emails are often misused and hence could become a deterrent to interpersonal relations*

Team Building

In consultation with the corporate HR, we organized a team-building session for all our staff for 3 days in a resort through various fun activities. The idea was to bring all the staff from both locations together to build relationships that was necessary to ultimately achieve the goals of the company. I had to do this amidst financial constraints as well as project execution deadlines, but I needed a starting point to move forward. We had a great session, and it was worth it since we never turned back from then, and our staff started working together with better understanding.

> *Making people meet and interact in a different environment improves relationships and thereby teamwork*

Suppliers as Partners

One of the issues I faced on joining this assignment was pending payments to our vendors who had supplied the material but could not be paid on time. This was mainly due to unfavourable payment terms we had entered with our customer, the Boiler commercial team. We could not collect our payment against our supplies because of the unfavourable payment terms and hence there was a cash flow issue. I approached my ex-boss who was my current customer and explained the problem. He supported me by arranging to give us some advance payments for the material already supplied to them. That was the time when he mentioned that he was instrumental in bringing me to this assignment, and he had to ensure my success for the good of the organization. When I started monitoring the overdue payments of our vendors systematically and ensuring payments were made on time, our Supply Chain head felt very happy about this. He started listening to me from then on as a loyal colleague saying that the old CEs were never taking care of the suppliers and he had to take the brunt.

> *Treat your supplier as a stakeholder and be fair to them to gain their loyalty*

I also used my past relationship with my Boiler colleagues for resolving many past commercial and payment issues, and these helped improve our cash flow to a good extent.

Relationship Building with JV partner

Our COO was in a withdrawn state when I joined. To establish a collaborative relationship, I started involving the COO in each major decision we took, and he slowly started understanding that I was transparent and had no ulterior motives to withhold any information from him. He shared a few of his bad experiences with the past CEs wherein he was cut off from information regarding the business. He was also very happy that I could get things done from the boiler team and that things were progressing. Slowly, he came around and started contributing to the business. While I had to interact with the staff belonging to his portfolios like Engineering, Purchase, etc. to deliver, I made him a party to our discussion thereby ensuring that he did not get offended for interfering in his work.

He was also peeved earlier that quotations that were submitted to the customer for prospective orders were not shared with him even though it was his portfolio, Purchase, who was giving most of the necessary inputs. I started sharing all information regarding financials with him. He kept complaining that we were giving away all our profit margins to the Boiler division, and this resulted in them making a profit and us making losses. I explained to him that the root cause of the problem was project execution not being done on time, and if we could stabilize the same, we could also make profits. Gradually, the teamwork between us strengthened and our business started performing.

> *It does not take much time to spoil a relationship, but it takes a lot of time and patience to restore the same*

Management Committee

We had a 4-member management committee consisting of 2 representatives as the COO and CTO from the JV partner and 2 representatives as the CE and CFO (Chief Financial Officer) from our end. We were supposed to be meeting every month and discussing various strategy-related issues, and table the minutes in the board meetings every quarter. The CTO who was also an expatriate reporting to the COO had joined recently and was a level-headed person. He cooperated well and requested not to disturb the established priorities to enable him to plan and work. When I joined, we did not have a CFO and hence we could not conduct these meetings. I was behind our corporate HR head since this was a key position for us to monitor the day-to-day running of the company, and the current employee who was filling in as standby was not experienced enough. Subsequently, we interviewed and selected a CFO who was very good - an asset to the organization. Usually, finance professionals, in my experience, always tried to be conservative in terms of protecting the resources of the organization. This gentleman was more receptive to business ideas and contributed well to the organization. Soon the management committee became a very good team.

In the meanwhile, I got promoted to the next level as **General Manager** and moved on to the next management tier in the organization. This was due to the fact that I had already cleared the MLP test to become eligible for the same.

Production Operations - Air Pre Heater

Our manufacturing facility had been making heater elements for Air preheaters for both Captive use and Spares. All the other components, including the housings of the air preheater, were outsourced.

Manufacturing Process

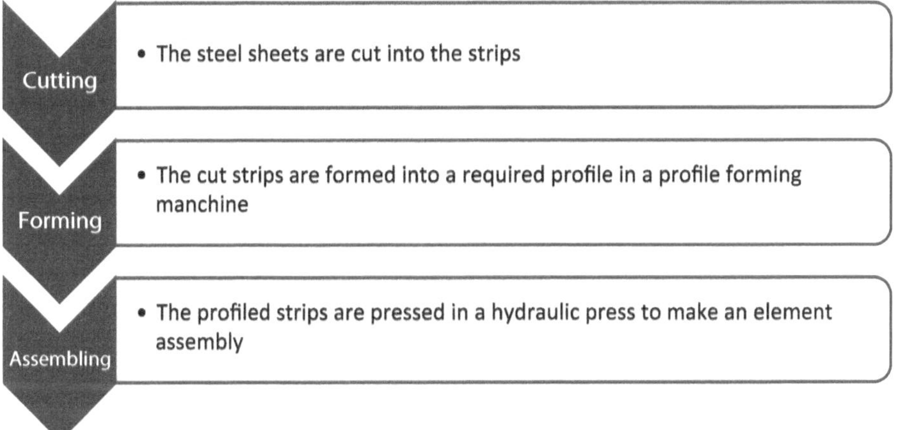

All the above operations were performed in a conveyor setup, and efforts were already being made to improve the throughput of the conveyor line.

We had excess capacity considering the orders on hand. When I questioned my Marketing Head about getting more spare orders, he explained that he was not able to match the competitor's price due to the following reasons viz.

a) Our pricing model was basic price based on full costing plus margin,

b) Transportation cost of the bulky heater elements resulting in not being able to compete in distant markets.

I instructed him to quote aggressively in future by considering only part of depreciation in calculating the cost to arrive at competitive pricing. This pricing strategy worked, and we started getting more spare orders. Once the capacity was getting fully booked including our captive order of preheaters, we were resorting back to full costing. This strategy had improved our cash flow as well as the bottom line. Thus, we had different strategies of pricing based on available capacity.

> *Unutilized capacity is always a burden on the company financially due to monetary loss in missing opportunities for money-making along with the additional burden of depreciation*

Axial fans

For axial fans, the critical components like the blades were imported from our JV partner as per the JV agreement while the housings and other auxiliary components were outsourced. We had a testing facility for our fans in the factory wherein the fan components were assembled and tested. The customer always insisted on testing one fan of each model to validate design and manufacturing. Since our execution was poor, there was enough spare capacity to test the fans. But once our execution capability improved, there was a queue for testing and the same had become a bottleneck. To resolve the same, we made a cross-functional team (CFT) of the Engineering, Manufacturing & Service teams to cut short the lead time of assembling and testing.

We were successful in this exercise as we cut short the losses during the activities of assembly and testing. The main challenge we then faced was when the test results were not satisfactory, and we had to rush engineers from our Engineering office to the factory which took an extra day. To resolve this, we transferred an engineering staff to the factory who, while working on Engineering, would also help with problem-solving during testing. He was also training a few service engineers for problem-solving in future tests. This had resolved the problem to a great extent, and we could improve our capacity for testing.

> *Always follow the practice of CFT when more stakeholders are involved in problem-solving*

Indigenization

Our Supply Chain Head was very good at negotiating with suppliers, including our JV partner sales team, and he brought us a good amount of savings in the imported components compared to the estimates he had given during quoting for the job. I was urging him for the indigenization of a few non-JV imported components like gearbox and motor. He made good progress regarding the same in consultation with our CTO. We also proposed to our JV partner to supply the imported components from one of their local units in India. We explained to them that this would make us competitive in the market and would also open a lot of scope in the spares market. They were seriously considering this strategy.

> *Indigenization is essential to survive in a competitive market*

New Markets

Our JV partner had bought one of his competitor's businesses and this had expanded our product portfolio to look for new customer segments in India. I recruited the engineer who had worked with me during my last assignment (and left to join our supplier due to his superior tooling knowledge). I leveraged him to visit all old power plants to investigate the possibility of servicing their spare parts requirements for their old fans which were currently in our product portfolio. We started getting inquiries, and we considered this market a gold mine. This engineer was also supporting our marketing head to focus more on fresh orders for fans and heaters along with the elements market for heaters.

> *There is always a new market to explore if you care to put in enough effort*

Negotiation for new orders

We also received new orders from our Boiler group. The negotiations for these orders were solely handled by me from the beginning. The negotiations happened with my ex-boss from Boiler, and he was fair and reasonable. He was a tough negotiator, but I tried to be as honest as possible with him regarding the costing. Initially, my COO was unhappy about such a sensitive exercise being handled all by myself. I explained to him that the advantage of my old relationship with my ex-boss would be lost if we did it otherwise. I had kept the management committee of the COO, CTO & CFO informed of my negotiations as they needed to be signatories to the contract. They gave valuable inputs, and I made the best use of them. The Boiler purchase group brought competitive quotations from our competitors to the table and my ex-boss used the same to drive the prices down. I countered with my argument of next-door preferential treatment and demanded a premium for the same. We both needed each other for discharging our respective roles successfully. We agreed subsequently on a fair price for each order which was a win-win for both of us, and my ex-boss kept on reminding me that he needed to make sure that I am successful in my current assignment.

> ***Be ready with an inventory of your strengths (Unique Selling Proposition) during negotiation***

Regarding order negotiation with other customers, our marketing head took the lead with me getting involved only in the final stages.

Financial Performance

All the above actions improved our turnover and profit, and after my second year, we had more than doubled our top line (Rs. 140 Cr plus). We made sufficient profit to recover our share capital to the original level of Rs. 120 crores, and further, we were also able to show an excess profit in the books. Our order book was also quite healthy to carry us through almost the next 2 years.

Change again

Due to my personal priority of needing to attend to my elderly mother, I requested my boss for a transfer to my hometown where our company had plenty of business establishments, and he promised to look into it. Within a month I got a call from the HR head of one of the divisions in my hometown for a meeting. He informed me that they might not have a Business Head position as I did not have the domain experience, but they might have a Manufacturing Head position. I readily agreed. He also mentioned that I might have to report to a person who is much younger than me in age. I said that I did not mind as I wanted the transfer desperately. I finally got my transfer order. In the upcoming board meeting, the news of my transfer was informed, and the directors understood my position. It was placed on record in the board meeting that my involvement turned around the business, and I was appreciated.

CHAPTER 16

MANUFACTURING AS A VALUE PROPOSITION

"Strive not to be a success but rather to be of value"
– Albert Einstein

The division I was joining was the biggest in the company with a turnover of close to Rs. 15,000 Cr. This division had five business units each catering to various parts of Power Transmission & Distribution including Substation, Transmission Lines, Utility Public Distribution, Solar Power & International. I joined the business of Transmission lines as **Head Manufacturing**. This business had three manufacturing units, with a total strength of 200 staff and 1500 workmen. While the business had a total turnover of around Rs. 4000 Cr., the turnover from the factories alone was approximately Rs. 1200 Cr (the balance turnover was from direct bought outs).

The product of this business was transmission towers made of galvanized steel structures made in-house in the manufacturing units along with cables, bolt & nuts, etc. which are bought out. Every newly designed tower was made as a prototype and tested in a tower testing setup located in one of the manufacturing units. This was done in the physical presence of the customer or a third-party agency to validate the design and manufacture of the tower. Only after the successful completion of the test to the satisfaction of the customer, clearance was given for bulk production by the engineering department.

The factory was a light engineering setup to handle high volumes of steel in terms of tonnage. The production process involved the fabrication of steel angle sections and steel plates. The operations performed were cutting, punching/drilling, notching & hot/cold bending operations followed by galvanizing (a process of zinc coating to avoid rusting).

There were 4 types of towers for every KV (Kilo-Voltage) rating based on the angle of installation between the towers. There was a wide variety of components involved for every type of tower. The combination of the number of tower types along with customer requirements for various KV ratings led to a vast variety of towers which in turn resulted in a multitude of components to be manufactured. The challenge for planning was to manage the production of such a wide assortment of components to complete every tower type on time.

The actual production output was 1,10,000 MT from all 3 factories against a total capacity of 1,20,000 MT. The requirement projected was close to 1,80,000 MT in the year I joined. The balance requirement was to be managed through external vendors either through outright purchase or outsourcing, subject to customer approval. The business was also in the process of enhancing the factory capacities to cater to increasing future needs.

Planning process

It was the central planning's job to allocate the load to various factories based on the demand raised by project heads of various regions and ensure timely supply from factories. Factories were focusing more on tonnage than tower completion. In the process, factories were ignoring towers with lesser volumes or components with lesser weight resulting in missing either a few towers towards line completion or missing a few components towards tower completion. Project heads were very unhappy about the way manufacturing units were dictating terms, and the concept of the internal customer was missing.

The Planning process (which used to be rolling planning for 16 weeks every month) used to be as follows:

Activity	When	Remarks
Meeting with stakeholders and Plan Finalisation	Beginning of Week 2	Organized by Central Planning
Determining Steel Requirement	Week 3	By units using Excel Sheets
Consolidation of steel requirement	Week 4	Done by Central Planning
Receiving Quotations from vendors	Week 5	By Central Procurement Cell
Approval by High-level Policy Committee (HPC) & Ordering	Week 6	To prevent malpractice in ordering
Production of RM (Steel angles and Plates)	Week 12	Lead Time by the supplier due to rolling cycle
Offering for Unit Inspection	Week 13	Other than self-certified Vendors
Offering for Customer Inspection	Week 14	As per contract
Despatch & Receipt in Factories	Week 15-16	Logistics arrangement by Factories

One of the main issues in the above plan was missing the rolling cycle by the steel suppliers who generally planned to roll their sections in ascending or descending order of thickness right from the beginning of the month. Placing the order in the 6th week resulted in missing the rolling of those sections which had already been rolled in the first 2 weeks and waiting for their rolling at the end of the subsequent month. This added to the delays in the supply of those sections.

As per the business requirement, the products had to be dispatched in 16 weeks (4 months), but the receipt of a few sections during the 16th week itself (as explained above) derailed the plan, resulting in a spill over of dispatches beyond 16 weeks. The Finished Goods (FG) must also be inspected by the customer before dispatch, and this also added to the lead time of dispatch. The project team would start receiving the FG only by the 3rd week of the 5th month (20th week), and till they received 100% material for a tower, they could not erect a tower and ended up erecting the tower only by the 6th month. Even if the supply of one steel section is delayed, the corresponding component could not be made and supplied. Hence the tower could not be erected.

All these issues resulted in a minimum lead time of 6 months from planning to erection. Any proto tower testing would add another 12 to 16 weeks to the above lead time resulting in an ultimate lead time of 9 to 10 months from order receipt. Lack of standardization (which is typical of any engineering job) had also added complications to the issue.

Lead Time Reduction

The first thing I did was to ensure that the planning meeting was conducted before the end of the 1st week itself. Due to this change, the lead time got reduced in the following manner.

Activity	When	Remarks
Meeting with stakeholders and Plan Finalisation	Week 1	Organized by Planning
Determining RM requirement & Consolidation	Week 2	Using software for steel length optimization
Receiving Quotations from vendors	Week 3	By Central Procurement Cell
Approval by HPC & Ordering	Week 4	By Central Procurement Cell

Activity	When	Remarks
Production of RM (Steel angles and Plates)	Week 8	The rolling cycle is not missed
Offering for Unit Inspection	Week 9	Other than self-certified vendors
Offering for customer Inspection	Week 10	As per contract
Despatch and receipt in factories	Week 11 -12	Logistics arrangement by Factories

All these tweaks reduced the lead time straight away by 4 weeks.

I also had a discussion with CPC about the possibility of ordering based on the vendor's rolling plan even at a marginal increase in cost (which of course needed to be approved by HPC) to shorten the lead time for supplying. This also helped us to get most of the sections faster than before and reduced the incidents of RM shortages in factories.

All the above steps improved the lead time to a great extent to a level of adhering to the dispatch plan by the 16th week.

As regards proto tower fabrication delays due to RM availability, I had instructed the factory to keep a minimum stock of various thicknesses in various grades even at the cost of inventory, which helped reduce the lead time significantly.

> *In every process, there is scope for improvement*

Review Mechanism

There was no systematic review mechanism happening in the manufacturing units. I decided to use the ISO review mechanism to improve the Manufacturing metrics. I discussed with the central Quality Head about ISO reviews in the plant. According to him, these reviews used to happen once a year just for formality wherein nobody bothered about using it meaningfully due to lack of conviction. To make the review more serious, I made a calendar for these review meetings to be conducted once a quarter in every plant (every month one plant usually in the 3rd week) and initiated the same.

In these reviews, we were covering all sections of the unit without neglecting any of them in all the plants. This used to take 1 ½ days. Initially, every section head was present, but I insisted that their respective deputy should also be present to have continuity for future reviews if the section head would not be available for the subsequent review for some reason.

Manufacturing Metrics

I introduced the following manufacturing metrics in the review meetings for periodic monitoring:

a. Safety - Frequency rate and Severity rate,

b. Productivity Fabrication - Kgs/Man Day,

c. Productivity Cutting & Punching – OEE for CNC Machines,

d. Availability of Utility – MTBF (Mean Time Between Failures),

e. Productivity Maintenance – MTTR (Mean Time to Repair),

f. Cost – Usage of End cuts in subsequent production,

g. Cost – Zinc Consumption per ton of Galvanising,

h. Cost – Furnace Oil Consumption per ton of fabrication,

i. Delivery – No. of full towers delivered as against planned,

j. Delivery – Average Lead Time for completing a predetermined quantity of every type of tower.

k. Quality – No. of customer complaints (including shortages from site)

Any parameter that is measured and monitored would improve

Zinc consumption and furnace oil consumption were already being monitored by these plants. I ensured that the good practices followed in any unit in achieving better consumption figures were shared with the other units. I was conveying in every review meeting that all manufacturing units belong to one team, and no more secrecy (which used to be the practice) to be encouraged or entertained between the units.

> *Knowledge management is a very powerful tool for improvement*

I also included a Critical Spares review to check whether spares were being missed for ordering under the blanket of budget and cost reduction.

Gradually I started calling all staff on duty during their specific section review. The seriousness of the message I had conveyed in these reviews got communicated to all front-line personnel, and implementation for improvement was on the way.

> *The involvement of front-line staff is the key to the successful implementation of any initiative*

Changing the Denominator

The above manufacturing metrics (i) & (j) forced the units to complete all tower types as well as smaller weighing components towards completion of the tower to improve the above indicators. With the introduction of these metrics, the denominator had been changed from tonnage to number of towers completed in everybody's mind.

Gradually, the outlook was getting changed from tonnage to tower completion resulting in the satisfaction of the Project Heads.

I also instructed that every shortage from the site should be treated as a customer complaint. This had led to the plant heads seeking confirmation through proactively seeking information from the site about the receipt of material without any shortage.

> ***Give primary importance to Customers, be it External or Internal***

Kaizen Initiative

I introduced and initiated the Kaizen initiative in all the units. Each staff member had to implement a minimum of one kaizen every month either by himself or as a team depending on the Kaizen. These had also become a part of the review to be presented in the form of number of Kaizens implemented by each department.

Theory Of Constraints (TOC)

To speed up the process of improvement, I decided to engage a consultant to help us in improving the factory's performance. I am a keen advocate of TOC (Theory of Constraints) and wanted to use this powerful tool to improve our factories.

I decided to engage this consultant initially in our unit 2 where the environment including the union was more conducive, whereas units 1 & 3 were balked down with union and infrastructure problems respectively. The consultant, after making an initial assessment of the unit, had chosen the Galvanising department to apply TOC. This was because galvanizing was the constraint evident from the inventory of black (ungalvanized) material lying in the plant overflowing into the roads.

Theory Of Constraints (TOC)- Galvanising Process

What is the Theory of Constraints?

In a chain of processes, a constraint is identified (this is usually the process where high WIP is awaiting). The identified constraint is given prime importance. All decisions regarding the other processes are subordinated to support the constraint process till the constraint moves to a different process and then the above steps are repeated. This is a continuous exercise that keeps increasing the throughput by removing one constraint after another and is hence immensely beneficial to the business.

Galvanizing Process

It is a 7-tank process involving cleaning/ degreasing, rinsing, pickling, fluxing, drying, zinc coating, and cooling. Once cooled, the finishing operation is done manually on the galvanized components to remove any excess zinc deposited on the same. We used to do around 70 dips in a day with an average tonnage of 1.75 tons per dip. Even during our regular reviews, I used to question this number since, as per their record, it took only 15 min per cycle, so we should have got a minimum of 81 dips considering the actual 22 ½ hour day (with ½ hour break per shift) and the standard 90% efficiency in any operation. The issues were ranging from start-up delays, crane breakdowns, etc. After taking various actions, we were improving and reaching an average figure of around 78 plus dips.

At this point, our consultant entered the scene and informed us that there is a possibility of almost doubling the current number of dips by focusing our effort on the actual dip process in the zinc bath and aligning all the other processes in line with the dipping process. According to his measurements, it took a total of 8 minutes for loading the material in the zinc bath, parking the same, and unloading.

Hence considering 22 ½ hours a day at 90% efficiency, theoretically, we should get little more than 150 dips.

At this point, a new Galvanising shop was also being set up in the unit to increase the capacity. The consultant asked us to stop the same, but we were too committed to back out. Still, we decided to pursue his idea in the current galvanizing plant.

This exercise of focusing on dipping precipitated a lot of issues in the Galvanising plant such as

- Lack of availability of EOT cranes for continuous loading,
- Poor Drier performance resulting in more parking time in the zinc bath,
- Variation in the crane operator's pattern of loading and unloading leading to different parking times in the zinc bath,
- Finishing process being done manually resulting in accumulation of components affecting further shifting of dipped components leading to stopping the process of dipping, etc.

The consultant suggested the following:

- Usage of the other crane used in the pre-treatment process for loading the zinc bath when the same was not in use while the components unloaded from the zinc bath were shifted to the cooling tank.
- Addressing the Drier performance through maintenance intervention to achieve the desired pre-dip temperature. This had prevented the extra parking time and ensured optimum dipping time.
- Installation of Timers in the cranes to standardize the crane operator's pattern of loading and unloading resulting in standard parking time in the zinc bath.
- Better hand tools to improve the throughput in Finishing resulting in clearing the components faster, preventing accumulation thereby ensuring continuous dipping and shifting.

All the above steps had increased the number of dips considerably. We could achieve up to 120 dips on some days, but we could not achieve the magic figure of 150 since crane availability continued to be an issue to load after every 8 minutes (like e.g., while the dipping crane itself was picking the material from the Drier tank). Soon, the number of dips started touching an average of 100 plus consistently with the result that the black material awaiting galvanizing got cleared and released a lot of floor space.

Now the constraint had shifted to fabrication wherein the current capacity was not sufficient to cater to the existing galvanizing plant. We also had to cater to the new Galvanizing plant which was commissioned and now was ready for production. The consultant started working on fabrication which was producing approximately 3500 MT per month through in-house fabrication facilities (The balance was being managed through conversion through local vendors).

TOC – Fabrication

As earlier explained, the fabrication setup consisted of CNC and manual punching for light sections/drilling for heavy sections followed by notching & bending of steel angle sections and plates.

Increase in Drilling Machine Output through standby tables

There used to be a lot of waiting time in drilling machines waiting for EOT cranes for unloading the completed steel angles and loading fresh material for drilling. The consultant introduced a standby loading table for each machine to enable us to keep the fresh material loaded and waiting to be taken up for drilling immediately after the drilling operation of the existing lot was completed. This increased the throughput of drilling machines by 25%.

Effective Utilisation of EOT Cranes through Relay out

The consultant also pointed out that material had to travel a lot to get the drilling done after the bending operation since the bending process involves heating the material in the furnace to facilitate bending, and all furnaces were kept in one corner of the plant for safety reasons. Changing the layout of a few drilling machines close to the bending area reduced the movement of material resulting in sparing the EOT cranes, which were now being used more for loading the material rather than the movement of material. This also had a positive effect on throughput increase.

Increase in Plate Production through Production Cell

Plates always used to be a constraint area and had created supply issues for the completion of towers. One of the reasons for the same was excessive handling, most of the time requiring the EOT crane. Any non-availability of the crane would result in a pile-up of inventory in punching as well as in subsequent processes like notching, bending, etc. as these operations were performed in different areas of the plant.

The consultant helped us to create a production cell by re-layout of the machines/ processes other than bending to minimize the handling. A production cell is an arrangement involving layout of machines in such a way to enable single piece flow of the components (not batches) through the production processes. Few hand trolleys were also provided to move the material between the work centres which reduced the dependence on the crane. These steps increased the throughput of plates by 20%.

All the above steps had increased the throughput of fabrication by 40% and the resultant in-house fabrication capacity had increased to approximately 5000 MT per month.

Visual Production Control

The consultant also introduced visual production control systems process-wise at the entrance of the shop. This would highlight any hold-up in any process that resulted in the accumulation of WIP to enable production to take corrective actions necessary to resolve the issue on a day-to-day basis. Similarly, he also introduced visual control boards for maintenance which likewise highlighted the long pending issues in maintenance for resolution.

Subsequently, I engaged the consultant in the other units, and he made some significant improvements in the other units in line with the above experience. As a company, we gained immensely from this exercise and that too on a permanent basis with a noteworthy positive change in work culture resulting in enhanced capacity and efficiency of operations. My quarterly reviews also ensured the sustenance of the same with a lot of focus on key production parameters with an increased level of productivity, safety, and quality at optimized cost.

Overall, engaging the consultant was the right path chosen as it had unveiled tremendous scope for improvement that we would have otherwise overlooked.

> *Solicit external help when you have too many issues on hand & want quicker results*

Cost Reduction

Another area our quarterly review had brought to light was the zinc consumption in each plant. We measure the same as% of the tonnage galvanized, and this was one of the key elements of our conversion cost (Cost involved in converting Raw Material into Finished product).

When I took over, this was hovering around 4.2% to 6% (the higher figure was in unit 3) across the plants. Benchmark figures from the competitors were as low as 3.8%. This meant our conversion cost was more by 0.4% amounting to Rs. 900 per ton (Zinc being priced at Rs. 2,25,000 per ton in India) even for the plant with the lowest consumption figure,. Considering our in-house production at 1,20,000 MT per annum for all 3 plants and the lowest zinc consumption figure, the increased cost of zinc coating alone amounted to more than Rs. 11 crores every year. This is without considering the higher figures for zinc consumption in the other 2 plants.

One of the main factors behind zinc consumption was the temperature of the material that was being dipped in the zinc tank. The temperature achieved was based on the heating efficiency of the Drier tank. If it were lower than the desired temperature, it would bring down the temperature of the zinc bath on dipping the material. This was leading to higher holding time of the material in the zinc bath till the desired temperature was achieved, thus resulting in greater thickness of zinc coating than specified. The other factor was the issue of achieving minimum thickness throughout the surface area of the bigger components (as specified by the customer) resulting in higher thickness of zinc coating in certain part of the component due to its geometrical shape.

During the review of the plants, we found that the Drier was not working properly resulting in not achieving the desired dipping temperature. We also found that the holding time in the zinc bath varied from one crane operator to another. Also in unit 2, the zinc crest which was removed was recycled then and there and added to the zinc bath resulting in lower figures to some extent.

The TOC steps taken earlier for improving throughput helped lower Zinc consumption as well in addressing the same causes. As regards non-uniform coating, various patterns of loading were tested to finalize a pattern to achieve minimum variation in coating the bigger components.

There was also a capital sanction to procure a zinc recycling plant for one plant but not acted upon. I managed to increase the sanction (through internal swapping) to procure and install 2 recycling plants in both units 1 & 2 with quicker delivery.

All the above efforts paid off, and we started achieving a zinc consumption of close to 4% in both units 1 & 2 which ultimately resulted in lower conversion cost.

Regarding furnace oil consumption in furnaces, steps were taken to ensure proper maintenance of all heating furnaces including arresting any leakage to prevent heat loss. These steps brought a significant reduction in the consumption of furnace oil used in these furnaces.

> *Focused effort always brings significant improvements*

Using Job Rotation for reducing Zinc consumption

I had a philosophy of never allowing an individual to remain in one function or one location longer than 3 years as this leads to complacency. I implemented this philosophy through Job Rotation & transfers for my team members. I followed this practice here also for all functions and all locations.

The lowest zinc consumption was from the plant in Unit 2 and was being supervised by a post-graduate in chemistry. This person was very knowledgeable and had taken a keen interest in bringing down zinc consumption. I used to challenge him during every visit, and he showed improvement each time. I transferred this person from unit 2 to unit

3. Here again, he played a key role in bringing down zinc consumption from the 6% level to around 4% level through rationalization of loads along with implementing the necessary actions, and this was achieved without even a recycling plant. I ensured that he was rated excellent and got promoted quickly to the next level even though he was not an engineer (Being an engineering company, non-engineers were not generally considered for quick promotion). Last I heard was that he was again transferred to unit 1 to stabilize and improve operations further.

> *Timely rewards always lead to improved motivation levels*

Changing the Head

Unit 3 was not performing well despite the regular reviews. The Unit Head had earlier worked in our business in a lower capacity and was taken back in the company to head this plant after getting enough experience in a different company. He was supposed to have attended to all the prevailing issues but was not acting at all. There were also issues of monetary irregularities in his plant with money being taken from contractors (for favouring work allocation and clearing bills) being reported from his plant. The contractors were all unhappy due to improper treatment meted out to them, and their loyalty was waning. While the Unit Head was a person with integrity, he was not effectively managing the plant.

This plant was already a big disappointment for the management with investments made for infrastructure albeit improperly. Many actions were pending, and no progress was being made review after review because of lack of leadership in either taking decisions or getting them executed. There was also the issue of getting the unit approved for production from one of our major customers who had listed a few requirements for approval, but none was getting completed.

All these factors forced me to look for a replacement for the incumbent. Since I was not authorized to take this decision on my own, I discussed it with my current boss (my young boss had been transferred to a different division) who was the Division Head. I proposed the name of the current planning head in unit 2 who was also the coordinator for TOC. Since my boss already knew the capabilities of this person, he readily agreed.

The change was made after asking the incumbent to resign (He was subsequently selected by my young boss for his current division for a different role).

Even before his joining, I arranged for a factory office inside the shop itself since the current team had an office away from the factory. On his joining, the new Unit Head along with his operating team moved into this factory office to have better visual control over the operations. To strengthen his hand and to develop a second line, I already transferred one experienced planning staff from unit 1 and the galvanizing expert from unit 2.

The new Unit Head had started taking a lot of actions including
- addressing the issues related to getting customer approval for the unit,
- Addressing the issues regarding contractors,
- timely decisions such as arranging transport for late hours,
- ensuring removal of the overgrown bushes in the raw material storage yard resulting in easy identification and pick up of RM, etc.

All the above actions resulted in the factory getting back in shape. He managed to create an environment that satisfied all stakeholders including the team of staff, contractors as well as the central planning cell by delivering on commitments made.

Challenges In Proto Assembly

One of the perennial problems of this unit had been to trace the components for proto assembly. They usually got lost for lack of accountability as well as storage in an open area in a muddy environment resulting in delays.

The new Unit Head devised a system of accountability through a proper handing over system that defined clearly who was responsible for when and what. This minimized the loss of components to a great extent.

The proto assembly was done in an open yard because of the size of the towers involved. This open area used to get muddy during the rainy season, and the working conditions were becoming horrible with the additional problem of small materials getting lost in the mud. The new Unit Head along with the help of the TOC consultant proposed and arranged to construct Cement platforms for doing this job. This not only helped the working environment but also helped to improve housekeeping and the overall ambience. This measure also prevents loss of material.

As already mentioned, the new Unit Head arranged to remove all old bushes in the open yard and unearthed a lot of old usable and unusable raw material. This solved the key problem of identification for stores to maintain physical stock and issue RM. But it raised the new issue of difference in book stock vs. physical stock which was now possible to take (this issue was camouflaged all along). We had to take approval from our Division Head for a one-time sanction to write off this significant difference in inventory citing that this old issue had been resolved once and for all.

The new Unit head also took a commendable initiative to plant saplings for a greener environment on the campus. He also created a Kaizen kiosk inside his factory premises to showcase the various Kaizen ideas implemented. This increased the motivation level of the staff to be more engaged in Kaizen activities.

Overall, he had made the unit presentable as well as well performing, and soon he was competing with the other units in all parameters. His move to the Plant Head position had become a masterstroke and solved a lot of problems for us.

> *Sometimes changing the head is the best solution to a major problem or for bringing new transformation*

I subsequently introduced throughput time from tower completion to line completion as a performance metric as suggested by our division head. This would ensure all tower types for a line in the required quantity would be available before the erection was started at the site. In turn, this would ensure good productivity at the site level. The above was only possible if there were no components of any tower type becoming a shortage due to missing of the component at the site (which was a frequent phenomenon due to strange site conditions).

> *We need to keep recalibrating our performance metrics and introducing new ones as and when appropriate*

Rolling Mill Performance

Unit 1 had a steel rolling mill. This mill was not performing in production, productivity, safety, housekeeping. Even basic lighting arrangements were not in place. The cost of production was high when compared to the landed cost of steel sections bought from external vendors. The main reason for the high cost was low-capacity utilization. The average production achieved per month was around 1000 MT as against the capacity of 2500 T. The reason for low production was frequent change over from one steel section to another at the whims and fancies of the Unit Head along with issues such as crane breakdown and conveyor breakdown. There were also frequent power outages resulting in shutting down of the unit affecting production.

The induction furnace for heating the billets was also not operating efficiently. This was due to frequent power outages resulting in repeated shutting down of the furnace, and plenty of leakages of heat in the furnace resulting in heat loss. This led to increased consumption of furnace oil which was also accounting for the increased cost of production.

The rolled sections, after cutting to the required lengths, were straightened in a straightening machine. Due to improper maintenance of the straightening machine, plenty of rolled sections were accumulated occupying valuable production space thus affecting further rolling. This created problem of the non-availability of straightened sections even though they were rolled.

The mill was headed by an old-timer who was technically strong but very poor in managing resources, and when questioned, he would always give excuses without offering solutions. I tried to improve his performance by listening to him and helping him with resources to resolve a few issues, but he was not delivering. I decided to replace him since that was the only solution left open to me.

There were a couple of smart young engineers in Central Planning. One of them was very energetic and outspoken and had a lot of ideas about factory operations. He had been initially transferred from

Unit 1, and he was aware of the issues prevailing in the unit. This engineer requested a transfer back to Unit 1 to take care of his wife's serious health issue in a reputable hospital located there. I transferred him to head the rolling mill in Unit 1 by transferring the old-timer to maintenance thus serving both purposes. I was confident that with his high energy and experience, this young engineer would bring the necessary changes to the rolling mill.

The young engineer wanted to shut down the mill for 3 weeks to address a few of the permanent issues such as leakage in the furnace, reconditioning the conveyor line by replacing a few key parts, etc. I sanctioned the same and asked him to simultaneously address the housekeeping and lighting issues during the shutdown. I also instructed him to clear the accumulated stock of rolled sections awaiting straightening to enable online straightening (as and when sections were rolled) in the future when the mill started again.

After 3 weeks, the total look of the plant changed with major work done in each part of the mill. The young engineer went to the extent of physically going underneath the furnace (not many would do it) to ensure clearing of all debris lying for ages. Such was his commitment to the job. He also cleared all accumulated sections awaiting straightening and arranged to store them vertically using storage racks fabricated from scrap enabling easy retrieval.

I asked the Planning Head of the tower manufacturing unit to treat him like any other external vendor and not to disturb him often in his planning. This reduced the frequent changeovers resulting in better production levels. I also pushed him to clear all old scrap material including old unused billets with the help of the Unit Head, and he showed good progress in the matter. He was able to achieve an average production level of 1500 MT every month, but we were pushing him to do better. He wanted the conveyor bed placed after the cutting machine to be changed as it had become very old and needed to be replaced. I was persuading our Head of Resources to manage the capital for the same, and he promised to look into it.

I was also urging the Central Purchase group to source cheaper raw materials (i.e., billets) for making the rolling mill more competitive, and they started working on the same.

In the meanwhile, our Division Head gave us a deadline of 6 months to make the rolling mill financially viable, or else have it shut down. I walked him through the various steps taken towards improvement, but he still stuck to his decision to review after 6 months. Subsequently after a couple of months, when he visited the plant to attend a presentation on digitalization initiatives, he visited the rolling mill and expressed satisfaction with the progress.

> *Sometimes changing the leader is the only solution for bringing new transformation. It is equally important to empower the new leader and support him in his initiatives*

Outsourcing

Outsourcing through the conversion model (Steel along with scrap allowances for process rejections and zinc would be supplied by us to vendors based on tonnage) was being followed to fill the gaps between capacity and demand. Our outsourcing with conversion model were of 3 types -

1. Local vendors were used to fill the gaps in capacities in specific work centres.
2. Customer approved vendors where the finished products were made. The finished products were dispatched directly to the site as a full set of materials for every tower type made.

3. An arrangement like the second type except they were brought back to the plant for onward dispatch to the site due to some vendor approval and customer inspection issues.

The outsourcing contracts were short-term in nature and there was no guaranteed outsourcing to the vendors beyond the term. The terms of the outsourcing were dictated by the finance department in terms of bank guarantees towards securitization of the value of the RM and zinc supplied. There were not many vendors willing to accept such terms for a short-term contract. Also, payments to vendors were made by an in-house third-party agency, Shared Services Centre (SSC) which held back the payment for even minor deficiencies such as a comma or dot missing in the document. Resolving such issues took time resulting in delayed payments which were also demotivating the vendors.

To resolve the above issues, along with the Central Planning Head who was also responsible for Outsourcing, I handpicked a few good reliable vendors and committed to their continuous business every year. I offered them one single contract every year covering all towers with different ratings. I also used the arrangement to get better financial terms. This also solved the problem of making contracts repeatedly every time for a new order, thus saving time in negotiations and getting approval from the bosses each time. Every year, we were demanding better financial terms in terms of zinc consumption, scrap rate allowances, etc., and we were gaining through some demands being agreed, if not every one of them.

Since the volume to be handled through outsourcing was more than 50,000 MT in the year to start with (remember the gap between our initial capacity of 120,000 MT and demand of 180,000 MT), this was equivalent to a virtual factory by itself. Soon the workload related to outsourcing picked up. Initially, help from our manufacturing unit near the outsourcing vendor was sought for inspection of RM & FG (finished goods), for determining RM requirements, and arranging logistics for transportation of FG to respective sites. Material accounting also had to be anchored to a nearby unit which meant maintaining 2 different material accounting within the same premises, one for outsourcing and one for their unit. There were a lot of issues due to the above arrangement with the units objecting to this new workload that was disturbing their operations.

Outsourcing Cell

After a year of the above arrangement, I mooted the idea of forming an outsourcing cell with a dedicated team and cost centre. Lots of doubts and issues were raised by the Central Planning Head and Finance team, but I persisted to clear all issues as this would relieve factories of the additional load and ensure their focus on their operations. We chose a location where most of our outsourcing vendors were located. Fortunately, we had our project office located in the same location, and we requested seating arrangements for a few staff. I transferred staff from all the units and requested staff from Finance who also obliged, and a new outsourcing cell was in place handling the same. Our central planning head continued to be responsible for this cell, and the above step brought a lot of accountabilities to the outsourcing function.

> *Having a separate identity is essential for performance and accountability*

Knowledge Management

I also started knowledge management sessions connecting all plants through video conferencing and making each factory present their good practices. Each month one section would be covered, and this even included maintenance as well as stores. Every factory/section head was instructed to follow the best practice in their respective units. Our Division Head was highly impressed with this idea. He insisted that each factory should be monitored for implementing the good practices, and we started doing so.

> *Knowledge management prevents the wasteful exercise of reinventing*

Improvement from the eyes of fresh Trainees

Each year our company selects graduates and diplomas in engineering directly from campus and allocates them to different businesses across divisions. Few fresh Graduate Engineer Trainees (GET) were allotted to us at our request. The usual practice is to depute these GETs to sections that need them. I had a different idea (I got this idea from a conference wherein the same was used by a new MD to reduce cost by 15%).

I deputed them individually to each section for 3 months covering fabrication, galvanizing, and maintenance. I asked them to record their observations with an open mind to bring out any improvements in any area in terms of safety, wastage reduction, manpower utilization, etc. other than learning the operations of each section. They were asked to present their observations in front of all Unit Heads and the corresponding section heads through video conferencing. There were a lot of valuable observations which led to further improvements in many areas of operations. I instructed the Unit heads to follow this practice in the subsequent years as a standard practice.

> *A fresh mind is unbiased in observations (the concept behind engaging consultants)*

Promotion

In the meanwhile, I was selected to attend the Development Centre Test (Management Leadership Potential Test renamed) to become eligible to get promoted to the next level. This test was conducted by external faculty unlike the ones for the lower levels wherein company trained employees were engaged. Only General Managers who were eligible for promotion were selected for this test and the pass out percentage is less than 5%. I once again dedicated sufficient time to prepare for the evaluation and successfully cleared the same. With this feat, I was promoted as **Vice President - Manufacturing.** Shortly afterward, I also got my extension of service for 2 years after superannuation.

Digitalization

The company had embarked on digitalization initiatives in most of its businesses and we were no exception. Competitions were held among various businesses as to how best digitalization was used to improve performances. A separate team of professionals for digitalization was formed at the corporate level as a central nodal agency to implement this initiative and carry it forward. Our division was also equipped with a dedicated digitalization officer. Recently, the company spun off the digitalization into a separate business by itself with the vast experience it had enjoyed across its multitude of businesses.

In our division, I undertook this initiative in Unit 1 in the following areas viz.

- Improve the OEE (Overall Equipment Effectiveness) of critical machines such as CNC cutting and punching machines,
- Improve the upkeep of equipment like EOTs
- Keep track of FG material for every project in our FG stores and site stores.

As regards the digitalization initiative for improving the OEE of machines, the main idea was to capture data regarding the actual time the machine was used during major operations such as cutting and punching. This was the exact time the machine was adding value to the business. All other activities like loading of material, programming of the machine, and setting up the job in the machine were essential, but they were not adding true value to the business. The old system of OEE measurement was including these non-value-adding operations in the actual calculation, and we were achieving around 70% to 75% as the OEE for these machines. The new system of measurement of OEE, considering only those activities that add value to the business, would force us to improve (decrease) the timings for non-value-adding activities. This would result in increased utilization of machines for value-added activities. We were using sensors for capturing data like amperage or voltage to sense the actual time of value-adding activity like cutting and punching.

The main challenge in the above undertaking was to be able to use the hardware and software used by CNC machines for collecting the data. But these were the proprietary of the machine manufacturer, and the machine manufacturers were demanding an exorbitant amount to furnish the same. Our central digitalization team was looking at alternatives to avoid incurring heavy charges, and they could manage to solve this problem in some machines through modifications.

Once the actual OEE was calculated in some of the CNC machines, it sent shock waves to the factory staff including the Unit head (I had already anticipated it). The OEE was in single digits ranging from 7% to 12%. One of the Unit Heads commented that he would lose his job if he showed such low OEE, but I explained to him that the new OEE figure was a reality.

> ***The Devil lies in the Details. Dig deep and use practical knowledge to arrive at true values, not just relying on theoretical calculations***

Subsequently, when our Division Head visited one of our factories to review the digitalization initiatives, he was equally aghast at these figures. I explained to him that this was the starting point for improvement as such data was not available earlier to act upon. I also explained that improving such OEE to a level of even doubling from the current level would have a great impact on the output of the machine. This in turn would avoid any further capital infusion towards the procurement of these machines for any further requirements. He was happy about the progress and asked us to work further to improve such OEE. I instructed the Unit head to form CFT (Cross-Functional Teams) to start working on these data to improve the actual OEE.

> ***Always subordinate all secondary processes to improve the value-adding process***

As regards the digitalization initiative on improving the upkeep of utilities like EOTs, we were in the process of making a central console to capture the data on wear and tear of important parts of the equipment through sensors installed at critical points and taking timely corrective actions. This data would be of great help in executing Predictive Maintenance.

For keeping track of FG, we were using mobile interfaces through our smartphones. The goal was for information such as tower-wise material availability to be available at the fingertips of all relevant stakeholders in both the factory and the site. This would enable dispatch of material tower-wise at the factory level with the same information being used to plan erection at the site. This was also supposed to improve tower-wise material planning and manufacture at the factory level. This in turn would ensure timely availability of full set of materials for tower erection at the site resulting in improved erection productivity.

This initiative was in an advanced stage of implementation. The main challenge lied in the identification of each component using bar codes at both factories and sites. These codes had to withstand all weather conditions to be able to be read by barcode readers in open storage in both places.

GOODBYE

While such futuristic activities were progressing at a rapid pace, I had to leave this assignment suddenly due to a personal reason – my aging mother needed my full-time physical support. I was extremely unhappy to leave the assignment midway through digitalization and other exciting plans for further improvements, but I had to. As last resort, my division head wanted me to continue in a consulting capacity at the least, and both of us agreed to look into such a possibility in future.

During my farewell, our division head openly acknowledged my contribution to the manufacturing operation by appreciating my initiatives and thereby highlighting how manufacturing can add value to the business.

Thus, I had put an end to my exciting career in manufacturing.

CONCLUSION

Once I got married and started having a family, I was trying sincerely to settle into a job to have longevity. But it never happened in the way I desired for various reasons. Looking back on my career journey of up and downs, I must conclude that I was responsible for each one of my decisions. But I must confess that I did not have any control over their outcomes. Many people around me played a part in shaping the outcomes be it good or bad. I accepted them in the right spirit and moved on. This only confirms the saying "Do your duty but leave the result to The Almighty". This is one of the key lessons that I want to impart to my readers through my journey.

They say it is initially hard to accept retirement after spending decades in pursuing your passion and being fully absorbed into it. However, I am very fortunate that my two little grandsons have kept my hands busy and my heart full. I have established some routines that help me spend time meaningfully. I am now free to travel, visit my loved ones, and pursue my hobbies and interests. This is another takeaway for my readers that it is in our minds to make the second innings as exciting and significant as before. Live every moment to the fullest. You may not get a second chance.

AUTHOR'S NOTE

I have read that life is a journey and we are all its passengers. I consider my career as part of one such journey. When I was in Boston, I was impressed by their local tours called **"HOP ON HOP OFF"** wherein any tourist can board and deboard in any of the tourist spots. I recently came to know that such an arrangement is available in our very own Mumbai. My career was almost like the above wherein I was changing my career at my will and wish like boarding and deboarding the bus, and hence the title of this book.

COMPILATION OF KEY LESSONS

General Management

1. Objective measurement is always better than subjective judgement. *(Page 18)*
2. It takes time to establish a new culture and we need to be resilient in launching a new initiative. *(Page 25)*
3. Every crisis always brings its own share of opportunities *(Page 31)*
4. Be with family on important occasions. It is going to be family that will be with you till the end and not the job. *(Page 32)*
5. Opportunity knocks at your door when least expected. Grab it with both hands. *(Page 36)*
6. Solving sensitive problems needs a plunge into it directly without resorting to delegation *(Page 37)*
7. Use informal channels for identifying and resolving issues *(Page 37)*
8. Certain solutions need additional efforts to bring an end to the problem. *(Page 38)*
9. Sometimes the solution to a problem rewards you with unexpected benefits *(Page 39)*
10. Do justice to your responsibilities in addressing all customers as each customer is important to the business *(Page 56)*
11. Make sure to live up to your commitments to increase your credibility *(Page 42)*
12. Sometimes the solution lies with the person who raises the problem *(Page 43)*
13. Asking for help (which many hesitate to do) helps *(Page 43)*

14. Patience along with perseverance solves all problems, and rewards would follow performance sooner or later *(Page 49)*

15. Sensitive information affecting working relationships should never be shared among colleagues *(Page 53)*

16. It is not qualifications alone but the experience that matters *(Page 55)*

17. Do justice to your responsibilities in addressing all customers as each customer is important to the business *(Page 56)*

18. Asking the right questions in a situation is one of the keys to problem-solving *(Page 57)*

19. Certain decisions need courage and conviction however unpopular the decision may be *(Page 60)*

20. Do not live with old issues. Resolve them one way or another *(Page 60)*

21. If you are fair and transparent, there is nothing to be afraid of *(Page 61)*

22. If you have confidence in yourself, you can always make a firm choice *(Page 61)*

23. A flexible approach leads to better solutions *(Page 66)*

24. Results speak louder than words *(Page 67)*

25. Sometimes changing the head is the best solution to a major problem or for bringing new transformation *(Page 163)*

26. Always do the RIGHT thing rather than a GOOD thing for long-term benefits *(Page 74)*

27. Never give in to pressure in any situation; Always stick to your principles and take the right decision *(Page 75)*

28. It takes real courage to admit mistakes in front of everyone, but it is worth it *(Page 79)*

29. The leader must take active participation in difficult assignments and follow through until successful completion *(Page 80)*

30. Leadership is all about doing the right thing with a long-term view rather than compromising for short-term benefits *(Page 81)*

31. Do not waste skill in mundane activities *(Page 85)*
32. Keep more people than required in high-skill areas even at the cost of increased headcount *(Page 85)*
33. Every customer is important and deserves equal treatment *(Page 87)*
34. Do not neglect any stakeholder irrespective of their status since any chain is only as strong as its weakest link *(Page 87)*
35. Cost reduction is a continuous activity *(Page 89)*
36. Evaluate the long-term implications of any decision which may give short-term gains. Always stand by principles and do not dilute them in the name of pragmatism *(Page 97)*
37. Good relationships always come in handy during times of crisis *(Page 104)*
38. Inculcate good habits among trainees right from day one *(Page 105)*
39. Deal with politicians diplomatically *(Page 106)*
40. Get into micro detailing for the execution of any project since it is the little things that get ignored and derail the project deadline *(Page 108)*
41. Be in continuous touch with the front-line team to understand the ground reality *(Page 114)*
42. Continuous networking is always beneficial *(Page 116)*
43. Set yourself as an example and show conviction in any initiative. Walk the talk *(Page 118)*
44. Any good initiative needs to start at the top *(Page 118)*
45. A good Leader always drives his team towards achieving challenging results *(Page 119)*
46. Always facilitate to ensure a successful implementation of any initiative *(Page 123)*
47. There is always a first time to starting a new practice *(Page 123)*
48. Follow Gemba (Workplace) principle to solve problems. Physical presence in a problematic area makes a big difference in a positive way *(Page 134)*

49. Discipline is the starting point for any journey towards a goal *(Page 135)*
50. Indigenization is essential to survive in a competitive market *(Page 141)*
51. There is always a new market to explore if you care to put in enough effort *(Page 142)*
52. Be ready with an inventory of your strengths (Unique Selling Proposition) during negotiation *(Page 143)*
53. Give primary importance to Customers, be it External or Internal *(Page 152)*
54. Solicit external help when you have too many issues on hand & want quicker results *(Page 157)*
55. Sometimes changing the head is the best solution to a major problem or for bringing new transformation *(Page 163)*
56. It is equally important to empower the new leader and support him in his initiatives *(Page 184)*
57. We need to keep recalibrating our performance metrics and introducing new ones as and when appropriate *(Page 163)*
58. Having a separate identity is essential for performance and accountability *(Page 168)*
59. The Devil lies in the Details. Dig deep and use practical knowledge to arrive at true values, not just relying on theoretical calculations *(Page 172)*
60. Always subordinate all secondary processes to improve the value-adding process *(Page 172)*

Factory Management

1. Fair treatment of unionized workmen always brings peace and harmony in the long term *(Page 44)*
2. Emphasize human safety & health and don't take things lightly *(Page 51)*

3. A safe work environment is always rewarding in terms of the high morale in the organization *(Page 51)*

4. Always keep the other party guessing in a critical union situation *(Page 59)*

5. Spares Management is key to Maintenance Management *(Page 66)*

6. Cost reduction through substitution should always be thoroughly deliberated before implementation *(Page 68)*

7. In-house subcontracting is always cost-effective provided the necessary infrastructure is available *(Page 68)*

8. Never compromise on Safety violations *(Page 77)*

9. 5S work culture results in not only good housekeeping but in good quality along with productivity and safety *(Page 78)*

10. There are many tools of Root Cause Analysis such as Why-Why Analysis (followed by Toyota) & 8D (followed by Ford) to resolve critical management issues involving quality, maintenance, etc. *(Page 79)*

11. We need to keep our ears to the ground in situations where industrial relations are strained and should anticipate adverse reaction and be prepared to face them *(Page 91)*

12. Treat contract people as stakeholders, give them due respect and recognition, and they become a strong tool in your hands to address any adverse extreme situation *(Page 92)*

13. Listening to people is key to developing and maintaining good Industrial Relations *(Page 97)*

14. Engage the maintenance team continuously by giving them assignments on improvement as they tend to become complacent during lean times of work *(Page 100)*

15. Proper spare management and equipment history card management are key tools for effective maintenance management *(Page 101)*

16. Ensure the most optimum and efficient usage of factory space including vertical space utilization *(Page 114)*

17. Ensure 100% visibility in factory operations *(Page 114)*
18. QC Tools are important for improvement in operations *(Page 124)*
19. Facilitate partnership between supervisors and workmen for a better work environment *(Page 125)*
20. Unutilized capacity is always a burden on the company financially due to monetary loss in missing opportunities for money-making along with the additional burden of depreciation *(Page 140)*

Production Management

1. Make workmen your collaborators rather than your low-level subordinates and this would bring wonders. *(Page 38)*
2. Good housekeeping always improves productivity *(Page 39)*
3. Look at your next shift operation as an internal customer and ensure a smooth handover *(Page 47)*
4. Never release all available resources at the same point in time. Ration critical resources *(Page 48)*
5. Have a healthy diet to work through various time zones in various shifts *(Page 49)*
6. Any shift engineer deciding on the shift has taken the right decision irrespective of others questioning the decision later based on hindsight *(Page 49)*
7. Never forget the human factor in any capacity calculation *(Page 58)*
8. In a conveyor line production setup, delegate all decisions to run the line continuously since line stoppage is a very costly affair *(Page 65)*
9. Process consistency is the key to consistent quality *(Page 74)*
10. There is good money in reprocessing and reusing, though often overlooked *(Page 90)*
11. Always ensure to operate your costly equipment with qualified personnel to get the best results *(Page 105)*

12. Ensure all operating staff are located close to their operations *(Page 114)*
13. Make every work centre as independent as possible *(Page 115)*

Delivery Management – Planning

1. Planning is the sole agency responsible for delivering on time *(Page 15)*
2. Planning is also responsible for gathering information internally & externally affecting delivery *(Page 15)*
3. Know about each of the processes/facilities related to capacity and process time *(Page 15)*
4. Plan for the bottleneck process/facility and subordinate everything else to the same *(Page 15)*
5. Plan for buffer capacity in the upstream process to take care of rush orders, quality rejection, etc. *(Page 15)*
6. Ensure staffing/automation in the finishing process for timely availability of the product for despatch without creating backlogs *(Page 15)*

Vendor Management

1. Always treat a vendor as a partner in your transaction with him *(Page 31)*
2. Be transparent with the vendor about any critical issues/situations. It would bring in trust in the long term *(Page 31)*
3. Guide vendors on how to reduce their costs through better quality and waste reduction *(Page 32)*
4. Always listen to them for any suggestions in the parts to be made and have the tenacity to take them up with your design section *(Page 32)*
5. Have one primary vendor with a major share and one secondary vendor with a minor share for any high-volume requirement to tackle any crisis *(Page 32)*

6. Correct the vendor upfront for any unrealistic price. This would avoid price revision and supply issues in future *(Page 32)*

7. Vendors are loyal to you if you ensure their payments are on time. *(Page 35)*

8. Price reduction does not necessarily mean profit reduction; rather it should come out of cost reduction *(Page 80)*

9. Internal subcontracting is always beneficial *(Page 88)*

10. Treat vendors as your supply partners and help them to address their concerns with whatever resources are at your disposal *(Page 99)*

11. Treat your supplier as a stakeholder and be fair to them to gain their loyalty *(Page 137)*

Stores Management

1. In a Stores Layout, it is a must to ensure "A place for everything & Everything in its place" *(Page 12)*

2. Ensure a Perpetual Inventory system and reconcile stock differences immediately *(Page 12)*

3. Ensure First in First Out (FIFO) for items with a shelf life *(Page 12)*

4. Carry out an aging analysis for non-moving and slow-moving items and take timely decisions on disposal *(Page 12)*

5. During disposal, do not wait to get a good price for the scrap, and in the process, waste your valuable storage space and run into an additional danger of good items getting mixed up with scrap and getting sold as scrap (This is how scrap dealers make good money). The faster we dispose of it, the better we are *(Page 12)*

6. Whenever a new greenfield project is set up, ensure that Stores is up and running from the first day since this will be of great help in accounting for project materials and helps in completing the project on time by ensuring material availability *(Page 12)*

Human Resources Management

1. Take care of the team members and they will take care of the work without any micromanagement *(Page 30)*
2. Informal get-together improves team building *(Page 30)*
3. Relationship building helps you to get problems resolved in the organization *(Page 35)*
4. If you do not address your weakness when you are young enough, your career would suffer when it mattered *(Page 35)*
5. Delegating responsibilities may not get the desired results unless supervised *(Page 40)*
6. The strength of an organization lies equally in its informal structure as the formal one *(Page 40)*
7. Collaboration can help solve issues when used tactfully while blame game spoils relationships *(Page 41)*
8. Informal relationships help diffuse many crises, and this is what is called as Managing Through Influence in the business world *(Page 42)*
9. Aggressive behaviour burns the bridges and never yields results or benefits. *(Page 50)*
10. Continuous assessment through recording of performance would lead to a fair and transparent performance appraisal process *(Page 51)*
11. Encourage your staff to make decisions and support them to learn from their mistakes *(Page 67)*
12. Be with people when they are in distress; this means a lot to them *(Page 69)*
13. Open transparent discussions always remove wrong perceptions and result in harmony both in professional and personal life *(Page 76)*
14. Empowering teams would release their valuable time for focusing on important issues *(Page 76)*
15. Be accessible to your team to listen to their problems *(Page 77)*

16. Ensure all stakeholders are properly trained before implementing an initiative *(Page 78)*

17. Right Empowerment motivates people and produces results *(Page 85)*

18. The best way to deal with interpersonal issues is through open discussions to vent out stakeholders' perceptions. Transparency always brings people closer and brings out any inner agenda *(Page 85)*

19. Focus on Human Resources Development for workmen. This would reduce the IR situation a great deal *(Page 94)*

20. Treat every employee as your internal customer and be fair to them *(Page 102)*

21. Be candid in explaining to the subordinate employees about their area of improvement, and do not shirk this responsibility because of the unpleasantness of the exercise *(Page 102)*

22. Keep a record of employees' performance throughout the year (Remember PPC in my earlier assignment) which would help assess the employee during the annual performance review *(Page 102)*

23. Spend enough time to ensure your career growth rather than only focusing on regular work, leaving everything to chance. This includes getting that extra qualification, attending training programs to improve your competency, etc. *(Page 109)*

24. Plant your ideas with team members in the early stages of enterprise to enable easy implementation *(Page 116)*

25. Open communication helps continuous employee engagement *(Page 117)*

26. Never allow a person to settle in a job since the same would lead to complacency *(Page 120)*

27. Quantification of skill leads to a better comprehension of the same *(Page 121)*

28. Facilitating continuous improvement and skill building on the job not only helps in the career growth of individual employees but is also powerful for improved company performance *(Page 121)*

29. Continuous improvement through self-contribution leads to pride & work satisfaction *(Page 122)*

30. Engage people continuously to keep their morale high *(Page 131)*

31. Emails are often misused and hence could become a deterrent to interpersonal relations *(Page 135)*

32. Making people meet and interact in a different environment improves relationships and thereby teamwork *(Page 136)*

33. It does not take much time to spoil a relationship, but it takes a lot of time and patience to restore the same *(Page 138)*

34. The involvement of front-line staff is the key to the successful implementation of any initiative *(Page 151)*

35. Timely rewards always lead to improved motivation levels *(Page 160)*

Computerization

1. Educate the stakeholders from end to end and make them process owners for their respective processes *(Page 24)*

2. Simplify the formats for data collection and design them in consultation with the respective process owner for easy implementation *(Page 24)*

3. Make a team of operational people to facilitate the implementation.

4. Identify siloed shop floor practices and institutionalize them if appropriate *(Page 25)*

5. Do not wait to achieve 100% perfection for implementation *(Page 25)*

6. Implement the system in stages in the logical chain of events from beginning to end and keep integrating the new process *(Page 25)*

7. Keep a subject matter expert to address bugs during the parallel run of existing and new systems *(Page 25)*

Knowledge Management

1. Use Quantitative methods using mathematical/statistical models to be more objective. *(Page 19)*

2. There are always opportunities available for improvement in every process *(Page 19)*

3. To be an effective industrial engineer, you need to be observant and analytical *(Page 19)*

4. Do not be afraid of failures as every failure is a step in the learning curve *(Page 19)*

5. Be passionate to defend your work in front of adversaries *(Page 19)*

6. Do not lose hope when your conclusion of a study and recommendation thereof is not accepted for implementation *(Page 19)*

7. Usage of modern management tools like Time Study etc. helps to improve the efficiency of operations. *(Page 22)*

8. Be updated with modern tools and don't hesitate to put them to use for better management *(Page 58)*

9. Always look for opportunities for improvement and use them to achieve the desired results *(Page 98)*

10. Implementing new ideas always has obstacles, but do not give up *(Page 105)*

11. Practical Application of Knowledge results in the culmination of the same *(Page 124)*

12. While computers are good for data storage and analysis, visual displays are good for awareness regarding the actual (present) vs target (future) *(Page 127)*

13. Improvement is a continuous journey. Ride the same to add value to the organization *(Page 129)*

14. Always have a separate set-up for process improvements to have focused efforts *(Page 130)*

15. In business, cash flow is equally important as profit *(Page 131)*

16. Always follow the practice of CFT when more stakeholders are involved in problem-solving *(Page 141)*

17. In every process, there is scope for improvement *(Page 149)*

18. Any parameter that is measured and monitored would improve *(Page 150)*

19. Knowledge management is a very powerful tool for improvement *(Page 151)*

20. Focused effort always brings significant improvements *(Page 159)*

21. Knowledge management prevents the wasteful exercise of reinventing *(Page 169)*

22. A fresh mind is unbiased in observations (the concept behind engaging consultants) *(Page 169)*

GLOSSARY

5S	A way of Work Discipline/Culture
8D	A Problem Solving Tool used by Ford using 8 steps
ABC	Activity Based Costing – A method of Costing a Product
BOM	Bill of Materials
CAPA	Corrective Action Preventive Action
CE	Chief Executive
CFO	Chief Financial Officer
CFT	Cross Functional Team
COO	Chief Operating Officer
CPC	Central Procurement Committe
CTO	Chief Technology Officer
CLIP	Committed Line-Item Performance
CNC	Computer Numerical Control
CVP	Committed Volume Performance
DET	Diploma Engineer Trainee
DG	Diesel Generator
ED	Excise duty
ED	Executive Director
EDM	Electron Discharge Machine
EOT	Electric Overhead Transmission

ETP	Effluent Treatment Pant
FG	Finished Goods
FOREX	Foreign Exchange
GET	Graduate Engineer Trainee
GM	General Manager
HDPE	High Density Polyethylene
HPC	High Level
HR	Human Resources
HT	High Tension
IR	Industrial Relations
ISO	International Standards Organisation
ITI	Industrial Training Institute
JV	Joint Venture
KV	Kilo Voltage
LT	Low Tension
Investment Casting	A method of making a product by moulding using wax of similar shape
JIT	Just In Time
Kardex	A system of Hard Cards for recording inventory
MD	Managing Director
MD	Maximum Demand
MLP	Management Leadership Potential
MNC	Multi National Company
MOU	Memorandum of Understanding
MS	Mild Steel
MT	Metric Tonnes

NC	Non-Conformance
OEM	Original Equipment Manufacturer
OEE	Original Equipment Effectiveness
OT	Over Time
PCB	Printed Circuit Board
PM	Preventive Maintenance
PPE	Personal Protective Equipment
Production/ Manufacturing Engg.	People who support Production through Process sheets, Jigs, Fixtures & Tooling
PV	Production Voucher
PQCDSM	Productivity, Quality, Cost, Delivery, Safety & Morale
QA	Quality Assurance
RCA	Root Cause Analysis
R & D	Research & Development
RM	Raw Material
SCM	Supply Chain Management
SHE	Safety, Housekeeping & Environment
SFC	Specific Fuel Consumption
SKU	Stock Keeping Unit
SOD	Small Order Department
Staff	Engineers, Supervisors & Managers
TPM	Total Productive Management
TQM	Total Quality management
USA	United States of America
VIP	Very Important Person

WCM	World Class manufacturing
WIP	Work in Progress
Workmen	People engaged in shopfloor to directly work with their own hands